SEOBRANDED

SEOBRANDED

What any Executive or Entreprenur
needs to know in order to master
search engine optimization
on Google, Bing & Yahoo!

Written by

Jesper Qvist

Contents

Library of Congress Cataloging-in-Publication Data:
Qvist, Jesper

ISBN 10: 0983897212
ISBN 13: 9780983897217

Printed in The United States of America.

First Revised Edition

0:// **Preface:**

SEOBranded is the complete essense and basic that any organisation should consider from day one of their existence and invest in, before they consider any other marketing investmens. The main reason why I want to share my knowledge about search engine optimization (SEO) is the fact that it is the most effective and cheapest way to attract new customers online. SEO is a strategy that every company should implement and pay attention to when communicating with their customers online. SEO is not easy but not very difficulty if you spend the time required, the return on investment would often be shown immediately and would increase your aware ness and sales by a high margin. SEO is not only for industry people but also for any one with an entrepreneur inside their body or the ones that are business owners should read this book and follow the steps to increase their profitability. This book is written to follow up on my first book "A Winner's DNA" which introduces you to a great number of tools that you should implement in order to increase your productivity and make more money. SEO is an important tool and the book is a part of the series a books that will follow up on "A Winner's DNA".

Jesper Qvist, September 21 - 2011
- Somewhere in the middle of the Atlantic Ocean! (Started this book on a Cruise from Copenhagen to Florida)

CHAPTER

1

"SEO must be a part of any organizations branding strategy!"

1:// Why SEO is crucial for any business

Search engines are often the best way to attract new customers online, which you of ten encounter in your own daily life. If you and your business are aiming for success online you should highly consider what great impact search engine optimization could have on your business and your bottom-line. The reasons are many, but it is proven if you are on the first page of the search results and among the first 6 results on Google, you will get the most attention and clicks to your site from possible customers. If you landon page two on Google, Bing or Yahoo! the odds are in fact that most customer snever find your site or business, even though your product and price might be more appealing for that customer. SEO is a tool and strategy that would heighten your com pany's visibility, competitive advantage and acquisition of new customers by a huge margin. We all on a daily basis search (Google) someone or something, and Googleling a customer before a meeting is commonin our world today. If you happen not to be in control of your SEO efforts when someone is Googleling you, you might encounter losses and damaging the image of your company if or when the wrong results shows

This book will teach you how to handle and effective gain a competitiveadvan tage in the rapidly changing market. SEO is a strategy that most companies do not see, know about or pay attention too, and by readingthis "Bible" you will learn how to strategize from a SEO standpoint and implement your strategy.

Why is Google so big and what is their story?

Google where founded in 1996 by two Stanford students Larry Page and Sergey Brin (not Bing). They did, as a part of their PHD studies, a study about the phenomena on how to gather information online and they realized that the more links a page has, which is linking into a site the more important this site was. Think about it in real life as well, the more people that refer something the more it sells (and being trusted). This phenomenon did Yahoo, MSN (Microsoft Search former Bing), Lycos, AOL and AltaVista not use and therefore did Google perform better search results on a short period of time after introducing their product for the world. The project form the research that the two founders did, ended up in being called PageRank (after Larry Page) and they filed a patent for it back then, which should expire soon.

> **Fact:** The name Google actually means the number Googol which is the number 1 followed by 100 zero's.

PageRank and Google did make a lot of sense since the more links linking into your website, the more "recognized" should your website be from others, which refers to a quality check and obviously would increase your rank on Google. Today the search engine got way more sophisticated since people started to trick Google with fake sites linking in etc. The complexity of Google is getting more and more compli cated, but there are ground rules and techniques that still count towards a better rating on Google.

The fundamental definitions: SEM, SEA, PPC, CPC and SEO

When speaking the language of the online industry and marketing industry, is SEM the overall importance when talking about SEO. SEM is Search Engine Marketing, which is covering all the activities when advertising on search engines and building a better ranking with SEO. Buying the right advertising at the right price on search engines and having the right ranking on your key words in organic search results is the most important factor when me suing your activities online towards conversations to sales and profit.

SEM is known in the two following forms:
1. SEA - Search Engine Advertising, "PPC - Pay Per Click" or "CPC - Cost Per Click"
2. SEO - "Search Engine Optimization"

When people or companies talk about SEA it is often referred to as PPC (Pay Per Click), Google AdWords or Microsoft Advertising. The main idea about it, is that you are bidding against your competitors for a search key word such as "Cruise" which can be many things, from a cruise ship vacation, cruise control on a car etc. Often generic words like these tend to get very expensive, but if you focus on words like Cruise Vacation Baltic Seas, will the companies that offer cruises in the Baltic seas prefer to bid this keyword since it tends to be more attractive and affordable. SEO on the other hand is all the functions of your online strategy that comes together into a ranking on Google, Bing or Yahoo's algorithm, which gives you a ranking on specific search key words. You need to buy the right keywords when you do SEA/PPC together with your keywords, that you ultimately are try ing to optimize on your SEO ranking for search engines. As an exam ple how a SEO ranking looks like for the search term Cruise (Figure 1.0).

Figure 1.0: Example of a search

Advice: Most people tend to click on the first 6-search result! This is what Google is considering the most relevant for you.

The importance of advertising on search engines: Google Adwords and Microsoft Advertising

As illustrated in figure 1.0, advertising is playing a big role of a search result. People tend to see the advertised keywords as a part of the search results, since the eye of ten tend to forget to focus on the part saying paid search results. What is great about PPC is that you only pay for each time a customer clicks on the link to your website. This for many online stores is proven to be the cheapest and most effective way to advertise your products. SEO is an important mix with PPC since companies often if focusing on SEO and paying the right price on Google for a keyword would be able to obtain a ranking on the paid first page, even though someone is bidding a high er price, since Google will take the most relevant sites as well into their algorithm. The basic of PPC is the fact that you are engaging in an Auction against your competi tors where you are bidding on the price for specific keywords. The question is what are you willing to pay per click each time someone clicks on your link. This is a tricky process, but Google and Microsoft is indicating their suggested bid price which is often a good indicator on the current price for any given key word you wish to buy. There is many factors determining your rank but your price and quality of the site is what in a combination is making your rank appearance on Google count in the end of the day.

Advice: Focus on SEO since this can decrease you Cost per click price in the end of the day, and you end up saving money on the same rank when buying PPC later.

SEO and SEM should go in hands!

It is proven when you combine SEO and SEA, your click through rate is way high er than focusing on either SEO or SEA alone. According to a survey conducted by Microsoft Advertising is the likelihood that a person clicks on your website is higher if you use both display advertising (Banner's) and search engine advertis ing combined the effect is higher on the click trough rate from your customers.

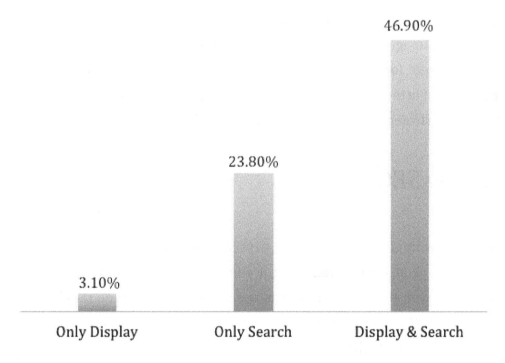

Figure 1.1: Source: Microsoft Advertising

This clearly illustrates that the combination of both SEM and Display advertising is prov en to have a higher effect on most users, compared to the strategies conducted on their own. Don't forget search engines are not the only channels that you should aim to use when attracting customers, but using other channels and combining those is proven to have the best results.

SEO is hard work

SEO is not the easiest task that you can start on today, but if you plan it right and do it weekly or every 2 weeks, your work is well paid of if done right. First step is to make your website search engine friendly which is of high importance when doing SEO. If your website is not build the right way, the crawler/robot (the way Google is gathering the sits to it's index) would have a hard time finding you and actually rank you higher than you are now. Websites containing flash have a harder time than others getting the right ranking, since the search engine do not read or understand flash, and the same case with images. Flash and Images can be tweaked to get a better ranking if you use Meta Tags, correct file names etc. for the images and flash files, you would be able to study how to improve those later in the book. SEO is first of all a great deal of work, when creating and implementing the strategy, but down the road the work that is required is less then at first.

Scheduling SEO

Scheduling SEO is important when your first implement and establish a strategy. Search engines look at your content and if you do not update your site with new content aimed as well at your search terms and users, your obtained ranking will go down and the ones that regularly update their content will receive a higher ranking. That being said this means that you should not spam your customers and the search engine with news, blogging etc. on a daily basis. Updating 24/7 can make the search engines believe that you are spamming them and this will give you a big hit in your ranking.

The SEO-Pyramid

I have developed a SEO pyramid, which takes the fundamental steps from Maslow's pyramid of needs. In the lower levels are the most fundamental parts of SEO. The higher you get the more advanced is SEO becoming. Everybody should start from the bottom up and follow the ideology of the SEO Pyramid.

The SEO-Pyramid is also a guideline for the level of SEO any organization are doing, and the different layers have different effects on the SEO process, which ultimately when you have studied this book will make clearly sense for you. If you follow the steps of the SEO-Pyramid the likelihood that you gain a competitive ranking on Google, Bing and Yahoo! is much higher than your competitors!

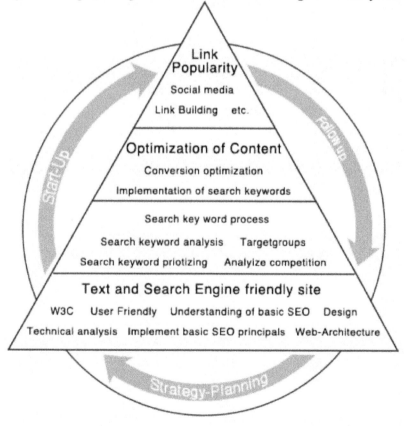

Figure 1.3: The SEO Pyramid

- **Text and Search Engine friendly site.** This is the step that anyone who wishes to obtain just a fair ranking on a Search engine should get done ASAP! You really need content on your website that the search engines can index and the easier and more related the content is for the search engine, the better ranking you will get in theory and practice.

- **Search key word process.** The second part of the pyramid is all about analyzing what key words gives you the highest effect. What search kewords are generating revenue and not just visitors; this is really what step 2 is all about.

- **Optimization of Content.** Step 3 is all about optimizing the content of your website, do not use search words to many times so you end up spamming the search engines, and not to few as well so you miss your position. Make sure that you analyze your site completely with tools like: Kiss Metrics or Google Analytics. Also it teaches how to structure your content from the importance's of Meta-Tagging, titles of the webpages and the content it-self. Overall this step is all about maximizing your search words in the content of what you offer your customers.

- **Link Popularity.** The final step of your SEO strategy is to build up a portfolio of links, linking in to your website and evaluate existing sites what value they have for you. Finally look at Social Media Optimization (SMO), which is all about Twitter, Google+, Facebook and blogging how it all can af fect your position on Google, Bing and Yahoo's organic search results.

Strategy planning, start-up and measuring the effect of your SEO strategy

The SEO Pyramid is what is linked to the "SEO Cycle" which is the strategy processt hat you would use of with the SEO Pyramid.

- **Strategy Planning**. This is the core element of your process, at this element you need to think about the long-term perspective of your business when starting the process. Furthermore should you look into new elements and optimize and plan new text, content and potential changes that will heighten your SEO initiatives.

- **Start-Up**. This is really about step 3 and 4 in the pyramid. Optimization of content and Link building is crucial to test before you make them public for the search engines.

- **Measurement of effects**. This element is very important since you would need to measure in to what effect the different search key words have on sales and visitors, and that way you can find different ways to optimize your website and SEO process continuously over time - and if needed change or optimize your strategy down the road.

Imagine you own a cruise line that has different ships and offers a huge variation of destinations for its customers. Every page on your website is describing the desti nations, the ships, what you offer etc. this is an overwhelming amount of data and information that the search engines would need to capture into it's index. You have cruises to the Bahamas, Eastern Caribbean, Western Caribbean, Baltic Sea Sea in Northern Europe, the Mediterranean, the Middle east, Asia and the Panama Chan nel as main destination but then all the destinations have different ships, dates and islands (ports) that you offer to visit. Now already here are the combinations of possible search keywords overwhelming and the potential search keywords that you can combine out of all your content. The main problem is that your website at this stage for your cruise line, is not optimized in it's framework and the way the site is designed to take advantage of SEO. When people search for a cruise to the Bahamas your site will not show up on the first page on Google since you missed out the opportunity of optimizing your site, so you rivals would actually receive all the business you might have attracted online, if you where smart. But had you focused on SEO for your online presence and sales, you might have ended up be coming more successful than your competitors (Who is smart now?). What a SEO strategy simply is, it is basically all about taking advantage, optimizing your on line presence the way you on a daily basis is trying to optimize anything else that touches your business. Analyzing your target groups needs and behaviors is more important than ever, and optimizing and tracking it online would not only heighten your SEO results, but it will also give you that edge of competitive advantage in your overall strategy. This edge will give you the ideas, data on how to differentiate and innovate faster than your competitors. SEO is the cheapest and by far the most important factor of marketing a company can engage in.

Did you learn the following?

☐ Do you understand what SEO, SEM, PPC and SEA means?

☐ Do you understand what the difference is between paid search results and organic search results?

☐ Do you understand what a SEO strategy is?

Own Notes:

_____

_____

_____

_____

_____

_____

_____

_____

_____

Part

1

Strategy Planning

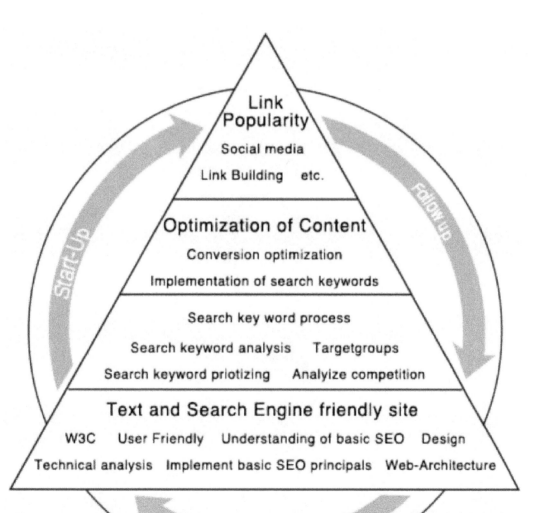

CHAPTER

2

"Start of with SEO the right way, avoid the common mistakes other do!"

2:// **Start off the right way with SEO**

SEO is, as you know by now a strategic tool and a strategy that no one wants to miss out on. Starting out creating a SEO strategy leaves out some very basic questions that you need to consider answering as a long-term strategy. This is due to the fact that you need to think long term for search engines, which is much better than short term, since this will secure your SEO status in the long run. When companies tend to change their online presence in terms of content, search keywords etc., they often suffer losses in their SEO position if not done wisely, which we will discuss later on. Questions that you should ask your self when starting thinking into to SEO terms are:

- Who is my target group?
- What is my target market and how is the market?
- Benchmark my online presence
- What resources do I have available?
- What can I expect from my SEO strategy?

- Who should run the project?
- Etc.

These are among the many questions you need to aswer in order to start off with you SEO Strategy.

Who is your target group?

It is extremely important to realize who is your target group, if we talk about our imaginary cruise line again. The questions will arise is the target group: senior citizens, young people, generation Y or X, the baby boomers etc. the reason why this really matters, is to know what these type of people we are targeting as you might have guessed. One thing we know as well is that people have different needs, price points and ways of discovering products online. Furthermore as you in chapter 3 will discover is the importance of knowing your target group, is really to identify their habits online in terms of search key words, which is the most important process when conducting SEO.

What is my target market and how is the market?

Knowing your target market is extremely important, but knowing where to find them and how to access them is what you really need to focus on. If you are targeting people that really do not use the Internet, then SEO might be targeted towards their family that will inform them about their needs. Would you as Disney a new player in the cruise market start to target senior citizens for their cruises or actually focus on families? these are simple questions that you should be able to answer about your own business, when someone wakes you up 3 in the morning and ask you!

Benchmark my online presence

It is important to benchmark your online presence in terms of what is your status at this moment. What is your rank on different search keywords, what does PPC cost you on search engines and is this, the best fit for your business. What does other channels offer you that Google, Bing and Yahoo! do not offer for your money. How does my competitors act, since you want to outsmart them and not copy their online strategy! If you use Google Analytics you would be able to measure most of your benchmarking online and you can ask your self, fundamental questions such as:

- What is the percentage of traffic to my website from Search engines?
- What search keywords are the visitors using on the search engines?
- What is the percentage of traffic to my website from paid advertising on Search engines?
- How long time are the visitors staying on your site?
- How many pages do the visitors in average see before leaving the site?
- What is the conversion rate of people buying products or contacting you?
- What is the cost of sales (conversation rate) from search engines compared to other marketing channels?

What are the available resources?

This is really a question about resource allocation in your company since SEO is at tracting different parts of the company into the process. You need to know how much you can either get help from departments in your organization or how much you can spend on hiring help from outside the organization. The reasons are simply that the bigger and more complex the organization is the more important is it that the employee comply and act after the SEO guidelines that you have set up for your organization. When doing SEO keep in mind that process require people with writing skills, web-design, link building, search keyword research, programming of the website etc. So make sure before starting that you have allocated the right amount of resources to the process (which only make sense to do!).

What can I expect from my SEO strategy?

When allocating resources from within the organization, the question will always arise what is the return of investment, what is the time frame and how does it impact our overall business. Well these are points that help you sell a SEO strategy to the organization since it is a long-term strategy that involves many parts of the company in positive ways. You will in the book learn how to understand the poten tial of SEO activities but overall the ROI will if your product is right and you know your business pay off many times.

Who should run the project?

Delegation of work and responsibilities are always important since a SEO process is combined of many aspects that you want to be on top of and delegate with your co-workers. It is important to delegate tasks among team members since the work load at times if you are alone with it can become overwhelming and it can kill of the great idea, in the end. Structure is important and you should make sure everyone in your team knows about:

- Who is responsible for what in the SEO project?
- What is the success criteria's for the project?
- What is the estimated time that is allocated to your work?
- When should the work or part of the work be done? - Deadlines are impor-tant!

The problem is when you need HELP

When your SEO project is about to fail or something goes wrong, then it is impor tant to know, that it is often due to lack of management and lack of execution of the planned strategy. Like any other project, you cannot be a Jack-of-all-trade and do everything, teamwork like in any other project and delegation of work is the essence of results. The reason why project tends to fail is that the project leader tends to loose the overall sight of the project. Many project leaders tend receive an overwhelming amount of Excel worksheet with work for the SEO project from team-members who didn't analyze the data but just collected it, these are many of the examples of small stupid things that kills a project. Details and analyzing is important and do make sure that you tell your team-members what to expect and then take the required action. If the team members do not know or have time to analyze the collected data, then ask a SEO-Consultant agency for help, and they will bring in expertise to finalize your project with you.

Examples of activities in a SEO process

This is a common example on how the outline for a SEO project could be formed:

Face 1: Research, Analyze and Planning:
- Develop a technical SEO analysis of the targeted website.
- Develop a search key word analysis to identify the right search key words.
- Link analysis.
- Benchmark analysis.
- Competition analysis.
- Set-up Targets, timelines and success criteria's.
- Develop an action plan.

Face 2: Implementation:
- Adjust and correct SEO related technical errors on your website.
- Evaluate the technical corrections.
- Search engine optimize minimum 75 pages (if you have that many).
- Write and publish at least 40 new SEO friendly text as content on your website.
- Create external link building to your website.
- Make sure your internal link building is working and optimized.

Face 3: Ongoing SEO:

- Always evaluate your SEO strategy.
- Measure the effect of SEO and report the results to your executive team.
- Always monitor search key words for improvements.
- Publish new content and texts that are SEO optimized.
- Continuously link building.
- Don't forget to follow up and improve your SEO strategy with the changes of the search engines!

Does your website exist on Google?

If your website is new, the odds that the search engines haven't captured your into their index yet is high. The reasons are many but often new or badly SEO developed sites are not always captured into Google's index, which is important in order to start a SEO project. It is really easy to find out if your website is cap tured into Google -- You simple just have to go to www.Google.com and press **"site:Yourwebsite.com"** for instance as the figure illustrates is www.JesperQvist. com captured into Google:

Figure 1.4: as you can see there is 30 pages added for JesperQvist.com on Google as illustrated

Just use the same guideline to check your site as I described and illustrated above. If your website do not show up on Google - then first of all you need to tell Google you exist by either two methods:

- The way websites often get captured into Google's index is from other sites linking in to your website, which is known as "link building" and therefore of high importance. This is actually the fastest way to get into Google's Index. Remember Google looks at sites with a higher ranking and award lower ranked sites with a better ranking if the higher ranked sites links to their site (The algorithm's way of trusting a site). This is the fastest way in some cases less than 24 hours to get accepted and found on Google.

- Secondly you can add your website on your own but this process is slower and I do not recommend you to do that, since it takes 2-6 weeks to get in dexed. You can add your site to Google on www.google.com/add_url.html

Test if your website is Google friendly

To test if your website is Google friendly the process is rather quick, and I recommend anyone to do it to check if their website have it's basic SEO principles in place.

1. First go to Google.com and type in "site:YourWebsite.com" to check what pages Google have indexed and how visible your site is.

2. Then click cache as shown in figure 1.5 below to see what Google have captured as shown is figure 1.6.

3. Then click on top on the text only version which is actually what Google is able to see, since it cannot guess and read how Flash, Pictures and movies are in real life if your site consist of that (But as shown later in chapter 4 that can in fact be improved). If you see text that you do not wish Google to index un der the text only version then there is something you need to change as well if things are not coming up as you wish, than you know what to add. If you look at figure 1.7 that is what Google in fact can see.

Advice: You can to Google.com and in the search field write "cache:YourWebSite.com" and see what Google have cached directly!

Figure 1.5: On Google you should click as illustrated above and then on cached on the right.

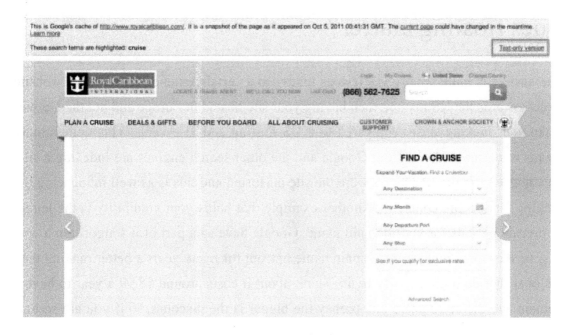

Figure 1.6: On the cached page you should click text only version to see what Google can see for your website.

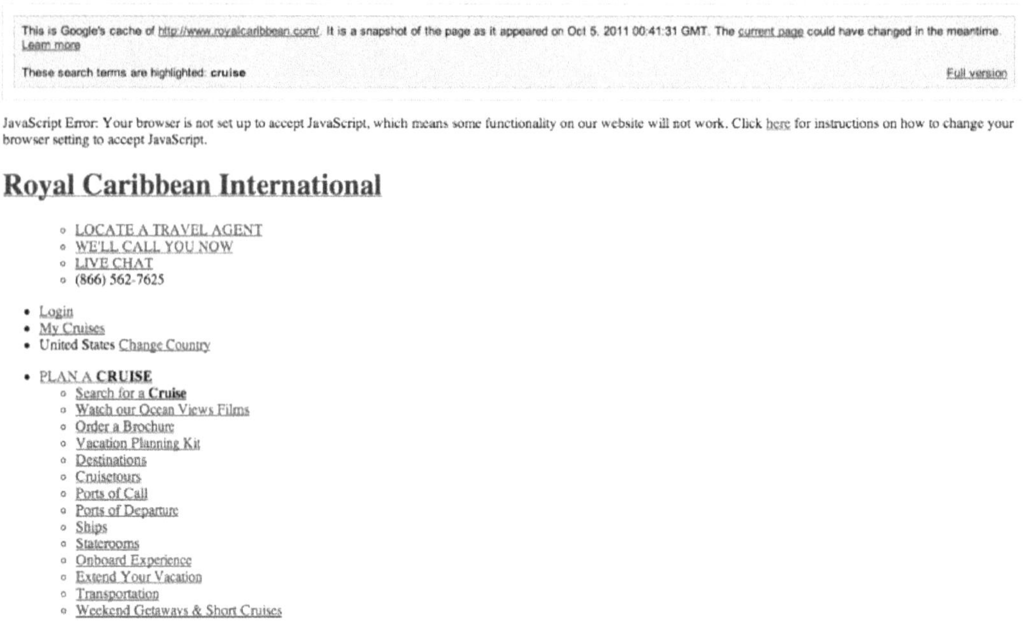

This is Google's cache of http://www.royalcaribbean.com/. It is a snapshot of the page as it appeared on Oct 5. 2011 00:41:31 GMT. The current page could have changed in the meantime. Learn more

These search terms are highlighted: cruise   Full version

JavaScript Error: Your browser is not set up to accept JavaScript, which means some functionality on our website will not work. Click here for instructions on how to change your browser setting to accept JavaScript.

Royal Caribbean International

- LOCATE A TRAVEL AGENT
- WE'LL CALL YOU NOW
- LIVE CHAT
- (866) 562-7625

- Login
- My Cruises
- United States Change Country

- PLAN A **CRUISE**
  - Search for a **Cruise**
  - Watch our Ocean Views Films
  - Order a Brochure
  - Vacation Planning Kit
  - Destinations
  - Cruisetours
  - Ports of Call
  - Ports of Departure
  - Ships
  - Staterooms
  - Onboard Experience
  - Extend Your Vacation
  - Transportation
  - Weekend Getaways & Short Cruises

Figure 1.7: Here is what Google really sees, as you can see is Royal Caribbean's website not done properly!

Does Hosting matter?

The answer is quite simply yes it does matter to a certain extend. If you run a website target towards the US market, then having your site hosted in Europe and not the US will make your ranking suffer compared to a US hosting and vise-versa. This quite simply means when the crawlers from Google and the other search engines are indexing a site, they notice ftom the IP address were the site is Hosted and this is as well influencing the ranking for specific countries. Another example that helps your credibility is the length of prepaid periods for your domain name. Google have as a part of it's algorithm a way to give sites that prepay their domain name upfront for many years a better ranking than the ones that do it on a yearly basis. Think about it costs around $8.99 a year to have a domain and the more years you prepay the bigger is the discount, so if you are serious and a sloppy person that could forget to renew a domain name, then it really makes sense to prepay it since you do not loose your "brand" and you increase your ranking as well.

Domain-naming tips

Your website address known as your URL is of high significance. Think about generic website addresses like Business.com, Sex.com and Casino.com they all sold for millions of US Dollars. Having a related keyword in your URL that relates to your products can help you to gain a competitive advantage in terms of SEO. There are some ground rules you can consider when choosing a new domain name. Lets say your company is named "123 Company" and your main business is cruises to Bahamas, well from a SEO point of view will a domain name like Cruise.com, Cruises.com etc. make more sense than 123company.com. Keep in mind that a domain should be short and relevant. Here are a few guidelines of what you should consider:

- **Keep the name as short as possible.** Think about your customers, if you domain is too long, then they might misspell your domain name and you will not gain that business. Also search engines might have problems with too long domain names, since they tend to rank them lower.

- **Avoid Dashes.** D-o-m-a-i-n names with dashes have a tendency to get a lower ranking, and people tend to write your address without the dash.

- **Focus on getting a .com and a local domain** if you do not do business in the states. Search engines tend to rank local domain names and .com domain higher than domain names with a different country code or .net etc. Why would you settle for a name that gives you a disadvantage and people tend to write .com or .local country domain since it is, in their minds.

Did you learn the following?

☐ Do you understand the principles of a SEO strategy?

☐ Do you understand how to check if your website is indexed by Google?

☐ Do you understand how to test if your website is Google friendly?

☐ Do you understand the project management of a SEO project?

☐ Do you remember that hosting and prepayment of your domain name matters?

Own Notes:

_____

_____

_____

_____

_____

_____

_____

_____

CHAPTER

3

"Search Keyword matters and you should concider is a cruise a vaction or Tom Cruise?"

3:// **Find the best Search Key Words**

Finding the right search keywords is one of the most crucial parts of SEO and one that you should spend more time on analyzing as a part of the strategy-planning process. For a Cruise-line offering pure trips from for example Miami to Bahamas. They should have focus on identifying what people might search for when looking for a cruise in south Florida. Maybe the density of companies targeting Miami-Bahamas is more competitive than Fort Lauderdale-Bahamas, which is nearby, and could be an easier target to gain a higher ranking on. But then again all the content would need to reflect Fort Lauderdale to give a higher effect, so finding the right search key words, as you will realize later on in the book is the most important process. This is simply due to the fact that it has to go hand in hand with the content to give the highest effect on your ranking.

Lets imagine you are on Google searching for cruise the combinations of words for a cruise can be many, from one word to 5 words ie.

- Cruise
- Cruise Bahamas
- Cruise Miami Bahamas
- Cruise all included Miami to Bahamas
- Cruise all included from Miami to Nassau
- Cruise for children
- Cruise for adults
- Party Cruise Bahamas
- Cruise without elder people

When you are analyzing the combinations that are available for your target group, it can be a vast number of combinations that you quickly can come up with as you see above. Guessing is often what companies do when they try to do 10% of their SEO strategy and they really don't have any idea over the complete picture. As you might see, the options of search key words that people search on in order to find your product and site can be endless and this is what really makes this part tricky. People might think they know their customers, but do they really? - Search keywords and analyzing what keywords are used from your customers and coming from organic search results in Google, is easy to figure out by using Google Analytics which might tell you more about your customers that you originally thought off.

Avoid the common mistakes others do!

I have chosen to gather the most common mistakes, which people tend to do in order to choose the right search keywords. My experience tells me that these mistakes can kill great SEO efforts and must be avoided at any cost:

1. **Guessing what is right instead of using facts and statistics!** This is often a huge problem that companies and individuals tend to do. People often think that they know what their target group wants, and from the simple fact they decide to skip analyzing their target group's behavior online. Companies tend to focus on specific keywords that people in their business community tend to use instead of using the words that their customers might use more often. Remember people online, do not always have the same knowledge about your business, and my advice is to set your pride of knowledge to the side, and focus on pure facts that your future customers would use!

2. **To use the same search keywords as your competitors.** Is very common that people go to their competitors website look at their "meta-tags" a code on the site that reveals part of their search keywords that they use. The problem is that you are not setting your self a side of your competition. You are rather following and copying them which often would give your a worse SEO ranking than them. Try to find something that is unique and sets you a side from them, this is what really gives you a better ranking on those search keywords. Finally maybe your competitor has chosen the wrong keywords for their business and why would you do the same mistake?

3. **Focus on one search keyword**, rather than focusing on search related sentences! People often tend to "lock" them self into one search keyword, which basically anyone do and that is making the competition even harder and worse. Focusing on a sentence that is related to a few important key words and related to what your offer is proven to give you a better SEO ranking.

4. **Choosing to warm search keywords.** This is basically words that everyone is trying to use and therefore the competition is extremely high.

5. **Choosing to cold search keywords**. This is the opposite of warm search keywords. Cold words are often weak search keywords, which you might think will differentiate you from your competitors but the problem is if the chosen words are to weak!

6. **Spending too little time on search keywords**. People as I described earlier tend to forget the significant advantage of what the right search keywords can give you.

Advice: Do a search in Google to see if the chosen search keyword in organic search results are related to your business area.

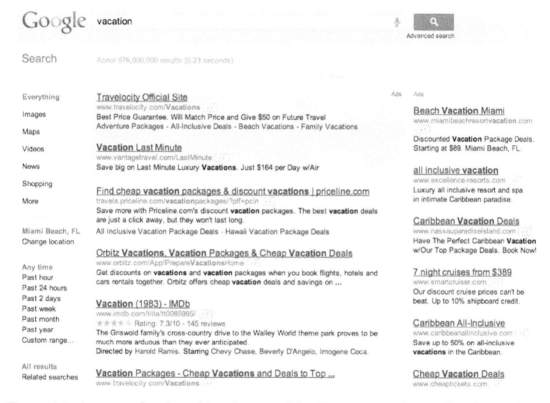

Figure 1.8: An example of combinations used for Vacation, such as: All inclusive, beach vacation etc.

Brainstorm techniques

Brainstorming with different departments from your company or people with a different mindset might show you that doing so, is a very effective way to gain new knowledge about the perception of your business. It is important to have different minded people in the process of finding and choosing the right search keywords. When doing a brainstorm by yourself (not recommended) or in a group. The main factors is to write all the words down to an excel sheet, since this makes it easier to upload later into Google for testing purposes and to organize it. I always suggest clients to spend 24 minutes on this exercise. The exercise is divided into 3 areas, which is aimed to heighten and give you and your group the best benefits of your brainstorm exercise and maximize the outcome:

1. **Overall Brainstorm session (10 Minutes).** The purpose of the overall brain storm session is clearly to identify what words are identifying your core business, and how can you see it from a broader perspective. You need to focus on finding words consisting of synonyms or direct keywords that relates to the offerings and products that your company wants to be found under, which consist of one or two words only.

2. **Find related words (6 minutes).** This is all about the Unique Selling Points (UPS) that you want people to search for and the related words that can be found in addition to the overall brainstorm part.

3. **Longtail search keywords (6 minutes).** Longtail keywords are important but also more difficult to find identify (described later in this chapter). They are related to a sentence of 3-7 words and they can be formed as questions as well. Customers sometimes search for an answer to what they want to buy, so identify these :)

What is my Unique Selling Point?

Your Unique Selling Point (USP) is often something that is extremely important to know in terms of a SEO friendly phrase to catch your customers. It is important that you know your USP and use it properly. Here are some suggestion on how to sharpen your USP:

- What are the common traits of your customers?
- What needs does your customers need to fulfill
- What is it that makes your product unique for your customers?
- What is the difference between your and your competitor's products?
- What problem do you solve for your customers and is there a solution to that problem?
- What is your product or brand value for your customers?
- What is your target market and how does your USP help?
- What does your price point and quality means for your customers?

What search keywords are my competitor using?

Finding out what keywords your competitors are using is quite easy, but copying them is not recommendable. It is always good to test them if you need inspiration and the best way to go is to go on to Google and search for a key search word identifying your business. Here are the easiest steps to do so:

- Go to Google and do a search on a related keyword for your business like "Cruises to Bahamas".
- Then go to the competitors website that describes your product the best.
- Right click on the website you went on to, click "show source code"

- When as shown in figure 1.9 you can see the source code for your competi tors website (not all is visible) but what Google can see and index is visible to you as well. Go to the part saying <TITLE>, <META NAME="DESCRIPTION"> and <META NAME="KEYWORDS"> here is their keywords and description that they use for SEO visible.

view-source:www.carnival.com/cms/fun/destination/bahamas/itineraries.aspx?subRegionCod...

```
    <!--Header Action Tag End -->

    <!-- styles for new header/footer -->
    <link rel="stylesheet" type="text/css" href="/cms/pageelements/2010/new-
header/css/header.css" />
    <!--[if lte IE 7]>
        <link rel="stylesheet" type="text/css" href="/cms/pageelements/2010/new-
header/css/ie7.css" />
    <![endif]-->

    <link rel="stylesheet" type="text/css" media="all"
href="/cms/pageelements/2010/common/css/style.css" />

    <!-- there should be no css after this head placeholder, so that the child pages can
override any styles in this masterpage -->

<meta http-equiv="Content-Type" content="text/html; charset=utf-8" />

<link href="../../../Styles/ccl08_css.css" rel="stylesheet" type="text/css" />
<link href="/cms/Styles/nav_08.css" rel="stylesheet" type="text/css" />
<title>Cruises to Bahamas | Bahama Cruise Deals | Carnival Cruise Lines</title>
<META name="keywords" content="3 day Bahamas cruise, Bahamas cruise deals, cruise activities,
activity cruises, cruise activity, carnival cruise itinerary, 4 day Bahamas cruise, 3 day
Bahamas cruises, 4 day bahama cruise, Bahamas itinerary, 7 day Bahamas cruise, 5 day Bahamas
cruise, carnival itinerary, 3 day bahama vacation, Bahamas itineraries"/>
<META name="description" content="Get great 3 - 6 day deals on cruises to Bahamas.  Our
Bahamas cruise itineraries feature fun-filled activities for the whole family. Book your
Bahama cruise vacation today!"/>
<script type="text/javascript" src="/cms/javascript/fancybox/jquery.fancybox-
1.3.1.js"></script>
<link rel="stylesheet" href="/cms/javascript/fancybox/jquery.fancybox-1.3.1.css"
type="text/css" media="screen" />
<link media="screen" type="text/css"
href="/CMS/PageElements/2010/common/js/fancybox/cclfancybox.css" rel="stylesheet">
```

Figure 1.9: Here is an example of the search keywords that Carnival Cruise line is using, and as you see Bahamas and Cruise is there both of them, which is why they came up on a Cruise to Bahamas search.

Long Tail keywords

The Long Tail was coined by Wired editor in chief Chris Anderson, in his book the Long Tail. The Long tail takes it origins from the Pareto principal, which is all about the 80/20 rule. The 80/20 rules in search are by the same principal as the method ology is in real life. 20% of search keywords bring in 80% of the traffic to a site in av erage. This phenomena means that 80% of regular searches are very hard to define and there can be a great selection of search keywords available. This is actually were you can gain many customers if you plan. In SEO are the Long Tail keywords, in it is basic all just search keyword sentences combined of 3-6 words. The characteristics of the Long Tail keywords are:

- Average 3-6 words in length.
- Each sentence generates only a few clicks a months.
- Usually not competitive sentences.
- Usually directly related to a product, question or information about it.

Furthermore should you consider that people generally on the Internet do not search for random information but rather specific information about something that they like! There are some characteristics of what people tend to search for online when talking about the broad search terms as the Long Tail keywords are.

- Product or Brand names.
- Product or Brand information.
- Product or Brand functionality.
- Product or Brand appeal.
- Product or Brand quality.
- Usefulness.
- Solutions to a specific problem.
- Information about places or industry terms.

What you have to remember is, with the long tail there is often a tendency to receive visits of higher quality, which often converts to sales and therefore is the group of keywords of high importance.

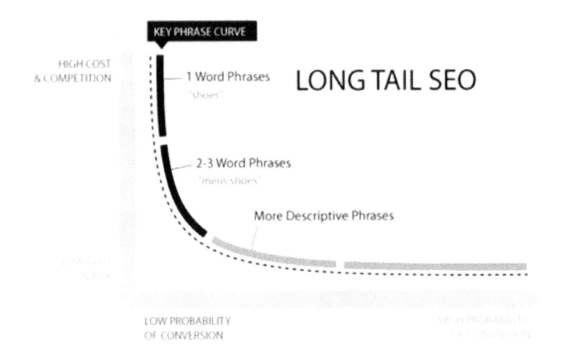

Google can help you to find the right search keywords!

Google consist of many tools that help business owners, finding the keywords that people tend to use for specific areas, which is quite simple to analyze and find on Google. When you write a search keyword Google will come up with synonyms for the word and actual related words from peoples behavior on Google related to the search keyword. You should always brainstorm with some collogues about possible keywords and these are to be used on Google to analyze what fits you the best. After a brainstorm follow these steps:

1. Go to "https://adwords.google.com/select/KeywordToolExternal" This is a tool that can help you as described. Please follow the steps as on Figure 2.0

2. Please insert the Captcha (the image) and write below the letters and or num bers, this is for Google to avoid robots from spammers to use this tool.

3. Click search and then start to analyze what is the right words for your business.

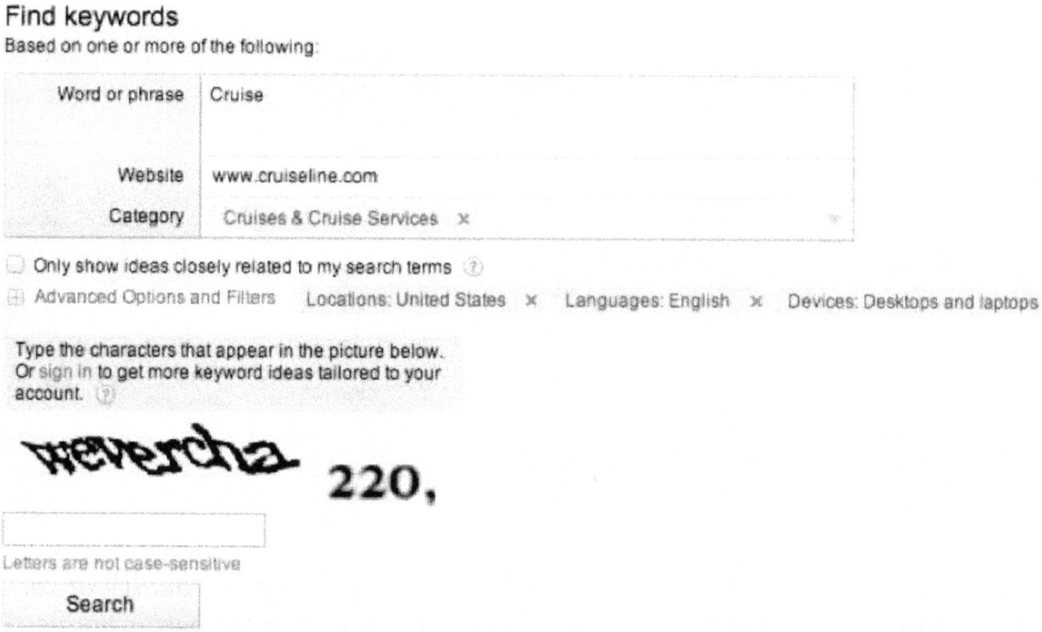

Find keywords
Based on one or more of the following:

Word or phrase	Cruise
Website	www.cruiseline.com
Category	Cruises & Cruise Services ×

☐ Only show ideas closely related to my search terms ⑦

⊞ Advanced Options and Filters   Locations: United States ×   Languages: English ×   Devices: Desktops and laptops

Type the characters that appear in the picture below.
Or sign in to get more keyword ideas tailored to your account. ⑦

wevercha 220,

Letters are not case-sensitive

Search

Figure 2.0: Insert your search word or phrase in the box as illustrated.

Search terms (1)			
Keyword	Competition	Global Monthly Searches	Local Monthly Searches
cruise		30,400,000	11,100,000

Go to page: 1   Show rows: 50   1 - 1 of 1

Keyword ideas (100)			
Keyword	Competition	Global Monthly Searches	Local Monthly Searches
cruise deals		550,000	301,000
disney cruise		823,000	673,000
cruises		20,400,000	9,140,000
carnival cruise		1,220,000	1,000,000
carnival cruises		1,220,000	1,000,000
last minute cruise		165,000	110,000
cruise vacation		74,000	49,500
cheap cruises		368,000	246,000
discount cruise		110,000	74,000
caribbean cruise		673,000	301,000
cruise lines		1,830,000	1,220,000
carnival cruise line		201,000	135,000
discount cruises		110,000	74,000
all inclusive cruise		90,500	49,500

Figure 2.1: Here is a great guide to see globally and locally (your country or target market) how many times people do a search on a monthly basis on specific words.

Use existing data to find search keywords

If your website have Google Analytics implemented, you will be able to analyze and see what search keywords that your existing customers are using to access your website, and this might give you a great hint on what words could be used. It is quite easy to access, all you have to do is to go to www.google.com/analytics and logon to your account. After that you will need to do the following steps:

- Logon to www.google.com/analytics and access your website.
- Click on "Traffic Sources" in the menu.
- Click "Search Engines" then click on "Google" or which search engine you whish to check.
- From here you will be able to see all the search phrases or words that your customers and visitors uses in order to accessing your website.

Focus on the easy targets!

Your customers do leave a great trace behind them, so why not use that statistical data that you track, to your advantage? With Google Analytics and other analytical programs that you can use for your website, are their options to setup goals and track the conversion rates of your customers and search words. This brings you to an important point if specific word or sentences/phrases provide a much better closing rate than others, why not to focus on that and use it to your advantage?
(your competition most likely do that, so why to leave out on that?)

How big is the competition for specific search keywords?

It is always easier and less resource heavy to focus on less popular keywords as you might know by now, but luckily does Google allow you to analyze the density of a specific search keyword as well. Finding the density on the specific keyword is im portant since, we have to keep your competitors in. The ones that have the keywords in their title would normally have a higher ranking than the ones that just have the words either on a text on the site or in their meta-tags. Meaning have a keyword in the title of your website would be a structure like "Cruises to Bahamas with Norwegian Cruiseline".

Remember always to bring the keywords first and then add your own brand last. Finding out as illustrated in figure 2.2 is fairly simple all you have to do is to type: "allintitle:Your Search keyword" on Google and you see the results.

Figure 2.2: There are 596,000 pages indexed with cruise Bahamas in their title

Figure 2.3: But as you see in the organic search results are the numbers different, in fact there are 48,600,000 pages indexed with cruise Bahamas.

How to analyze the density on search keywords

Analyzing the density could be different than when you specify your keywords from Cruise (456,000,000 results), Cruise Bahamas (48,600,000) to Cruise Bahamas 1 day (3,620,000) so narrowing down the titles on your website and using the right keywords is as you see of high importance. The reasons are simple, it is far easier to obtain a higher ranking on words that has less competition, since you would assume some competitors are investing in SEO as well.

1. **Check the title-tags density.** As you learned with "allintitle:your search keyword" is the methodology a very important way to measure the density of SEO improved sites, that will have the keywords in the title for the desired site.

2. **Deep analysis of the density of the selected search keyword.** You would need to spend time analyzing the landing pages of the top ranked sites, which words they use, what is their title-tag (you will learn about it in the next chapter) and what backlinks do they have, which are linking back to their site, which is another reason for their ranking?

> **Advice:** Remember a search keyword like Cruise might seem like the best keyword for the Cruise industry, which is in most cases are corect.
> The only problem is when you are competing with 456 Million sites for

Use Google insight for insight!

Google Insight is another excellent tool to use when doing SEO. All you have to do is to go to www.google.com/insights/search and you will be able to see insights from people search habits historically, geographically and what news that is big in the specific search word industry, like the Cruise Industry. When checking the search word "cruise" it is interesting that Tom Cruise the actor, is showing up as the third most used searched keyword phrase with Cruise in it, so be careful. What is really great about Google Insight is:

- You can do Relative search keyword trend for a keyword and do comparisons between other keywords to check the popularity.
- Find top related search keywords and what are the hottest rising related keywords at the moment.
- See the category based top search keywords and categories that are based on the hottest rising searches (and overall top 10 rising searches if needed).
- You can find category based keyword search volume trends, and the relative growth of a keyword compared to its category.
- Find countries, states, and cities where a keyword query is popular.
- You can also mash up many data points, like celebrity searches in Miami in the past 15 days.

What is great about Google Insight is in fact that are able to compare search volume etc. for two key terms or more that you might wish to analyze as possible search keywords.

Figure 2.4: As you can see above is the ranking or search terms that people use when searching cruise, resort and vacations. Where they search for which shows that Florida is the most popular place in the US for cruise and Resort, which we all knew deepest inside ourselves.

Google Trends for trends

Google Trends is another great tool to find and help prediction of future trends or ongoing trends. Google trend is focusing more on the media aspects and it shows what are happenings right now or are posted in the most media regarding your se lected search keyword.

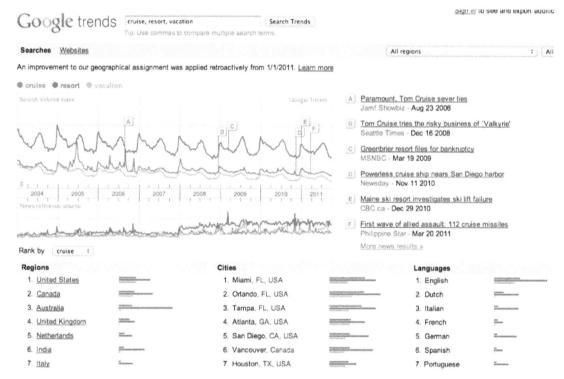

Figure 2.5: Shows that under the search keyword Cruise is Tom Cruise popular and what related to, of a bigger impact online. This is great information for industries to follow up on once in a while on trends in their industry.

Tip for picking your search keywords

1. If you are new into SEO, I would recommend you to pick search keywords with a lower density, which in the short run would give you a better ranking, and then later on focus on the more competitive words.

2. Focus on search keywords that are related to what you offer or are trying to sell online, do you miss that is most of the work a waste of time.

3. Finally try to use your analysis and then search use the right keywords.

Did you learn the following?

☐ Do you know why you should use Google keyword tool?

☐ Google Insight, what are the benefits?

☐ "allintitle" what does it mean, and what effect does it have in SEO?

☐ I understand Long Tail keywords?

☐ I know how to brainstorm properly for SEO?

☐ I know how to check my competitors keywords?

☐ I know what my Unique Selling point is?

Own Notes:

_____

_____

_____

_____

_____

_____

_____

_____

Part

2

Search Keyword process

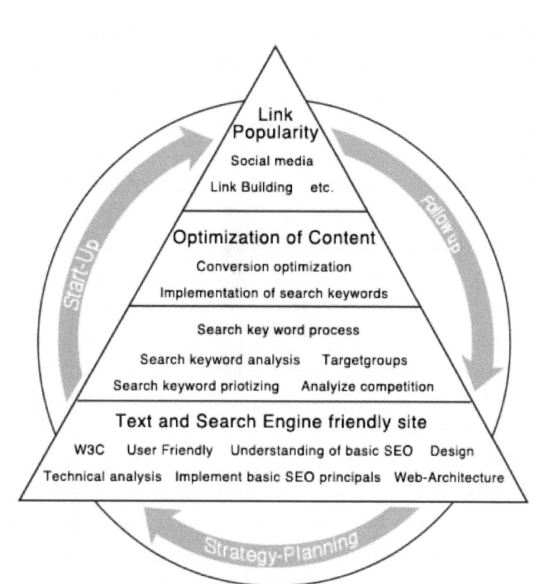

CHAPTER

4

"If content didn't matter would New York Times Exist?"

4:// Effective content optimization

Optimizing your content is extremely important in order to gain a great SEO ranking. Finding you search keywords and plan the strategy, is simple what we call the planning process. When we initialize the start-up process, is the focus quite different, now you need to take action! Take a look into your whole online presence and optimize all parts of it so Google, Bing and Yahoo! can read and understand what you want your customers to find and do it right in order of accomplishing your goal to gain a higher rank. Remember websites have different types of con tent that can be optimized with simple methods, compared to how you might do it today. Images, Videos, PDF files, Sound files, documents etc. you need to take a different approach following you overall strategy to optimize all parts. In SEO terms all of this is called "on-page optimization" since you are optimizing what is directly on the webpage.

Rethink you website

Remember when people access your website, they either get in by typing www.Yourwebsite.com or if the customer is not aware of you or just searching for product/services that you happen to sell or offer they might end up coming into a product page. This makes your website more unique, since people will access your website on any given page and that is you landing page in any given situation. Op timizing landing pages is essential and do remember when you Google for a Book you most likely end up on the product page on Amazon or Barnes and Nobles but not their FrontPage. Think about your website structure as upside down, if you did your SEO correctly you would wish your customers would arrive on the product page and they would buy, and that is often what SEO does!

The traditional way of thinking a structure, people come in on the FrontPage and click down through the categories to the final product:

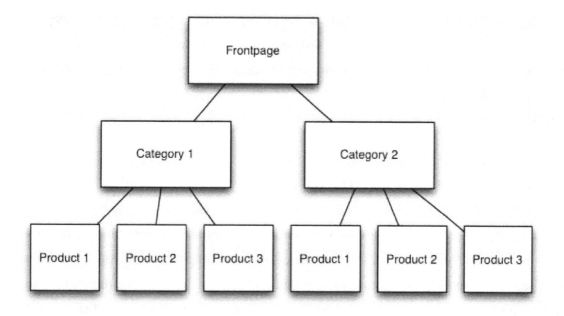

Figure 2.6: Traditional thinking of a website structure

When people find you through a search engine would the world be opposite:

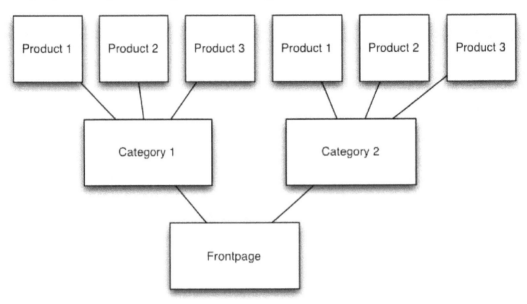

Figure 2.7: How you should think about the hierarchy of your website!

Keeping this in mind, you should rethink the process and focus on the product pages in terms of SEO first, since you want to sell more. Think about the long tail theory from the strategy face, people often tend to access your product page, and they might never see the FrontPage so remember all pages are "FrontPages" or what we call landing pages.

Optimization of landing pages

Landing pages are important to optimize since all pages are possible landing pages on your website. As you might now some pages are more important for you if more than one page on your site is fighting for the same place on Google. But there are a few things to keep in mind, getting more traffic are not the same as getting valuable traffic. Attracting traffic and optimizing your landing page is two of the most important ele ments in landing page optimization

It is easy to check your own website for and which site is ranked the highest under a search keyword. Here is an example how NCL.com (Norwegian Cruiseline) have done. As you can see all you have to do is in Google to write:

"site:yoursite.com search keyword"

and all your sites will show up that are ranked with the search keyword.

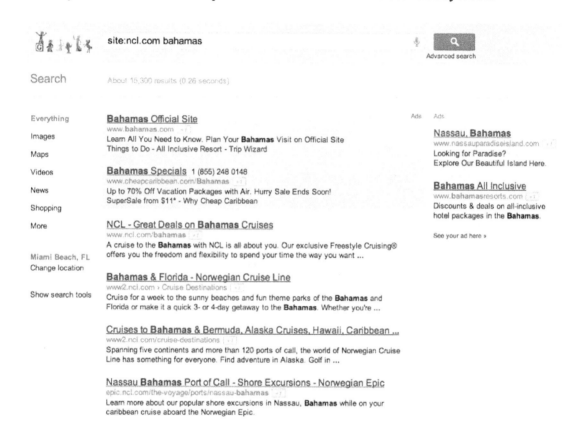

Figure 2.8: Here is a good example, NCL have managed to get their information site about Bahamas as number one, which shows the cruises that goes to Bahamas below.

If NCL.com had another site than they wish for to come up as number one under the search keyword Bahamas, would they need to change the content, and meta-tags on the specific site, and improve which ever site they wishes that receives a higher position. Furthermore should they convert their keywords to sales, which is something you should monitor from Google Analytics as well.

Optimize each landing page with a search keyword

The idea is quite simple if you are a cruise line and sell cruises all over the world, then you might want to specify for the search engine on each page. Examples are many! Lets make an example: You do offer cruises to "Bahamas" and another customer do a search for a "Cruise to Mexico" then the keyword should be differentiated on each site in order to attract the right people to the right site. If someone whishes to take a cruise to Mexico and lands on the Bahamas page, you most likely not get that deal, but if they hit the Mexico cruise set - thats your target. Remember if you wish to be a top ranked SEO site on Google etc. then focus on having all pages fine tunes for them, in order to index you higher.

Remember to optimize the Page Title for each page

When people do access your webpage it is important to optimize the page title in order to get the highest SEO ranking. As illustrated in the example from Norwegian Cruise line is an example of the right way to do it. They have the search keyword in the title, url and meta description which is important for each page to have in order to gain a competitive advantage.

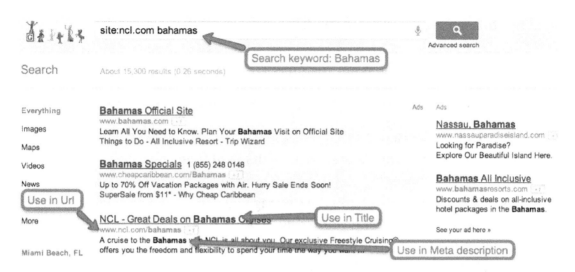

Figure 2.9: Great example of how NCL.com have optimized their site to it fullest in terms of Search keywords in the title, url and meta description.

When you want to optimize a process it is quite easy in terms of the title, in basic HTML is the part of the code you need to change the following:

```
<head>
<title>You company name and search keyword or phrase</titlte>
</head>
```

If you follow these instructions you would be part of the way, the meta description and url optimization method will be described later in this chapter. Remember the page title is what you see as the title of the page when you click on a link on Google and when you enter a site the title is playing a deeper role in the customers mind that you might think.

Great tips to keep in mind when optimizing your page title:

- Remember to make each page unique, otherwise your SEO ranking would suffer and you will miss out customers.
- Use your primary search keyword in the title for the related product or ser vices.
- Do not use more than 70 characters in the Title, Google will not index more when they show it on their search results (and then your message is not brought out).
- Use search keywords first in the title tag and if you need or have space for it insert you company name in the end of the title.
- Remember to use small and capital letters for a better attraction even though it is grammatically wrong to start the word with a capital letter!
- Always if possible use phrases or words that make the possible customer click more easily like buy, sale, book, download, free etc. something that make them want to click.

Meta Description

A Meta description is the part on a Google search that describes the site you might want to click on as illustrated in figure 3.0:

Figure 3.0: Illustration of a Meta Description on Google

Each page needs an optimized meta-description to tell the customers what a search on Google offers them or if your page is satisfying what they expect to see. Often people tend to forget to make a meta description and then random text from the page that Google is indexing will show up, which often do not have the same effect at all for you and your website.

What is important is that you should avoid duplicating the Meta description for each page, since the description is quite obviously would end up being the same for all pages. Another thing that are important to know is that the Meta description is not a part of your ranking on Google, which means this purely describes the site for the user when they see their search results. One note is that Bing still uses Meta Descriptions in ranking, so on Bing it counts more. Remember on Google the length of text that you can see is never longer than 150-160 signs so try to stick between that numbers with your Meta Description. Any time quotes are used in a Meta description Google cuts off the description. To prevent Meta descriptions from being cut off, it's best to remove all non-alpha/numeric characters from Meta descriptions. If the quotes are important to include they can be changed to single quotes rather than double quotes to prevent truncation. Here is an example how the code looks like in HTML:

```
<head>
<meta name="description" content="Add your description here. This will often show up in search results.">
</head>
```

Meta Keywords

Meta Keywords is located in your HTML code and here is a great place to use your search keywords from you keyword analysis. Remember Google do not add any specific ranking from your Meta Keywords optimization so spending too much time here is really not worth it, but it does count on Bing and Yahoo! so if you aim to rank high on those search engines you could pay some attention to your meta keywords.

```
<meta name="keywords" content="search keywords" />
```

One rule of thumb when doing Meta Keywords it is important to prioritize them so the most important ones is first and then divided with commas the less important ones come later.

Make your images readable for Google

As we all know an image is better than a thousand words and this is truly something we all use on a daily basis to illustrate our thought clearly. The problem is that Google cannot read images unless you give them a hint, which will help you to gain an optimization. The information you can give search engines all lies in the HTML code and most online blogging systems, CMS systems etc. already have this function build in which is to give the image a description, so when you have hold your mouse over the picture it shows a description of the image that Google and you can read. Here is an example of how the HTML code would look like:

```
<img src="images/picturename.jpg" alt="YOUR PICTURE DESCRIPTION HERE FOR SEO PURPOSES" />
```

Headings

Headings are actually of higher importance than you might think and most online CMS, Blog, Ecommerce systems etc. have headings build in for you. The reason why headings is important is that search engines sees these headings as a hierarchy of what is important and the higher ranked the heading is, the more important. So when a search engine optimize your website remember to have the SEO keywords in the heading of the site, since Google, Bing and Yahoo! will emphasize more and those keywords than the regular content.

69

The headings are as many other parts of SEO done in the HTML coding of your website. The headers have a structure where H1, H2, H3 would be the name of 3 different headers, and obviously number one is more important than number two, and number two is more important than number three.

Here is an example of how the headings would look like in HTML code:
- <h1>Your Heading here</h1> (Most important header)
- <h2>Your Heading here</h2> (Second most important header)
- <h3>Your Heading here</h3> (Third most important header)
- Etc.

Best practice advices for headers:
- <h1>Cruises to Bahamas</h1>
- <h2>Cruise to Bahamas on or free style ships</h2>
- <h3>Bahamas cruise's is all inclusive and a perfect way to travel</h3>

As you can see in the first header is the focus on the keywords Bahamas cruise, while in the second and third level is the focus changing towards the story and it keeps the main keywords.

Tagging of words

It is important to know that Google actually look at a page like you do with your eyes when we look at the text and content. Words that are written in "bold", "italic" or are in "• bullet points" are considered more important for Google since they stand out. Keep in mind to emphasize and to have the SEO words as the ones that are standing out, so that creates a competitive advantage for you online!

Here is an example how it looks like in HTML code:

- <b>Bold words</b>
- <i>italic word </i>
- <li>Bullet points</li>

One reminder don't use keywords to, to much in situations like these since Google could potentially look at you as spam, since they would try to avoid people taking advantage of strategies like these. Finally never use-underlined words, since these would for the end user are looking at them as hyperlinks!

Optimization of media files

When you Google something you might have noticed that it is not only websites that come up in your search results anymore. But actually Google includes text files such as Words, PDF files, images, videos etc. as a part of your search result.

Figure 3.1: Here is a great example of different media, which shows up in the search result.

The great part about media files is that most people tend to overlook SEO in that part of their only presence. This makes it far easier for you to obtain a better position on Google, Bing and Yahoo!. Remember that search engines are rapidly changing how they categorize search results on the result page as shown in figure 3.1. The good new is that the blend of new media is rapidly changing the landscape. Twitter, Facebook, Docstoc, Slideshare and YouTube are among the live trending results that might appear together with other media, which who all will fight for the highest SEO ranking. But at this point is the integration is on and off with social media on Google, Bing on the other hand have exclusive right to show Facebook in the search results and do not expect that to happen on Google, since Microsoft bought into Facebook in the early days.

Remember when you upload and showcase PDF documents, pictures, videos— Remember to think SEO in the file name, so you enhance your online position. Media files might be a different strategy you would consider for the high-density keywords, you might have no chance to compete on, and that way you can gain a better online presence.

Advice: Think about a search keyword analysis on your media files as well, and go back to chapter 3 and look into your analysis.

Gain a better ranking through your media files!

Do you happen to have a website with a majority of media files available then media optimization is a must for you, and you might happen to gain some cheap points in the search engines from that process. Look how hotels can benefit from direct booking on the landing page on Bing!

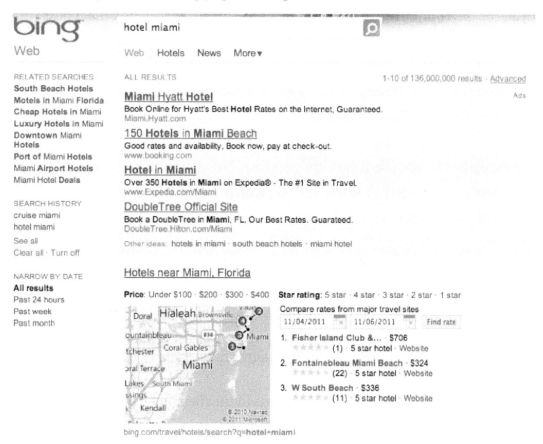

Figure 3.2: here is an example of how a hotel can benefit and make money from Bing directly on the search result pages.

Optimize your documents

Since your company most likely have documents uploaded for multiple purposes, you might consider optimizing them as mentioned earlier. The reasons is simply you want people to find them and do business with you. Examples of document that you can SEO optimize are many, but here are the most common file types:

- Microsoft Word (.DOC or .DOCX)
- PDF files (.PDF)
- Microsoft PowerPoint (.PPT or .PPTX)
- Microsoft Excel (.XLS or .XLSX)

Documents are like simple HTML they need a file structure to be optimized for search engines. You need to think SEO keywords in the text that you upload, use the right types of headers etc.

Here are the best practices options that you should apply:

- Make links from the documents back to your website, especially if it is product descriptions, it might enhance a sale and optimize your SEO effort.
- If your document is longer than one page, try to have the most important keywords on the first page to gain a better ranking on Google, Bing and Yahoo!
- Try to have the file name use keywords in the file name with dashes like: "cruise-ship-bahamas-description.PDF".
- Use bold or strong typing on the important words in the document (remember search engines looks at these words as more important).
- User headers in the document like (h1, h2, h3) structure.
- Use the functions in Word, Excel etc. and add Title and Meta descriptions so the search engines can rank you higher (often done by File and then properties).

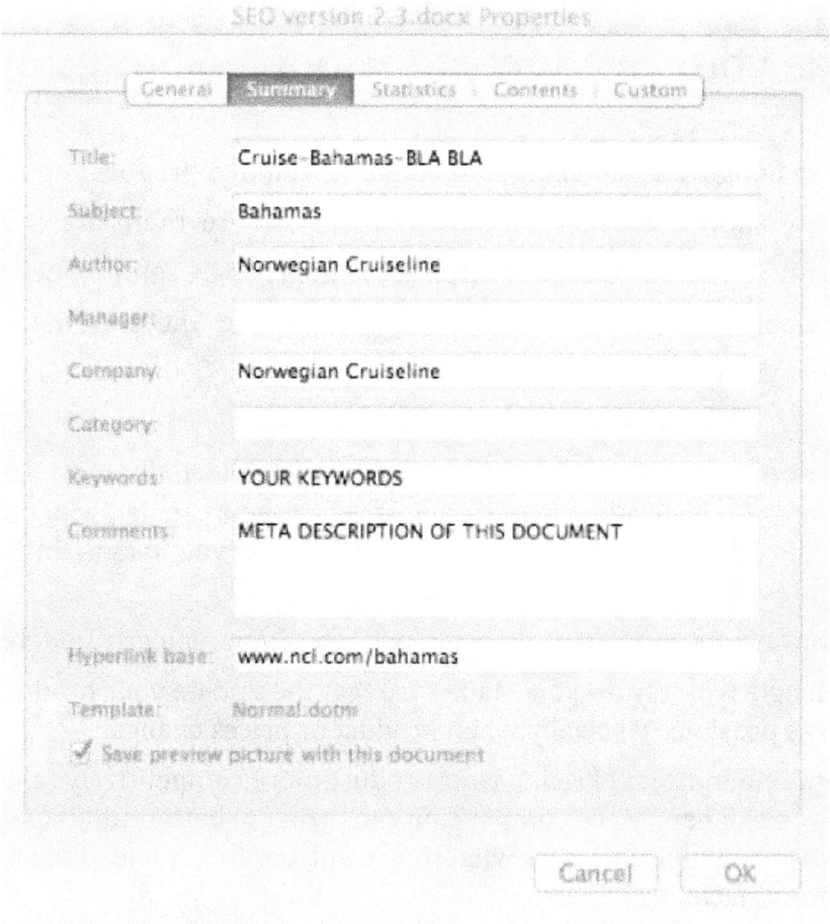

Figure: 3.3: Illustration of a word optimization.

Optimize your products for Google Shopping

When you use Google for searching info about or to find a product you might have seen that they show a category called shopping, where there are a variety of products with different prices (http://shopping.google.com). The Shopping category on Google is a bit different compared to regular SEO and there are some key points that you need to remember:

- **Title and Description.** It is just like regular SEO, including relevant keywords in the product title tags and descriptions can help you rank. A strategic, keyword-rich description can also allow you to rank for long-tail key phrases not targeted in the title tag.

- **Fresh Data**. As you know, the never and when you regularly update your site Google will reward you. Make sure that the update your product feed as often as possible, especially when product or prices change.

- **Capitalism matters!** Pricing your product more competitively (cheaper) than your higher-priced competition can promote better rankings—Google's way of giving the customers what they want and this is one of the most important factors.

- **Too much Data**. While keyword stuffing is generally considered black-hat (meaning don't do that). It is important to provide the customers and the search engines with as much information about your products as possible—not just the minimum information you think is required in the Google Shop ping set up— this will help your product to rank for a variety of queries.

- **Reviews**. We all know that positive reviews can greatly enhance a brand's reputation and sales. The only problem is when we are talking Google Shopping and SEO is there a significant difference between where the review appears from in origin. When you think about it, it do make some kind of sense that Google considers reviews (both negative and positive), which is an indicator of how big a brand is, with more reviews signifying greater brand awareness appears. The problem is that Google actually heighten sites with a great SEO ranking better as review sites than sites with a low SEO ranking. It does make sense since they consider better sites as more correct, and they have a bigger authority online.

Get your site on Google Local!

The reason why Google local matters and are clearly more important than most people might think. Is simply, think about when you use your smart-phone and press Google Maps and type dentist, Burger Bar etc. the locations that have added them self to Google local and maps by location would be the ones that shows up and get the business, especially for offline business. Forgetting to add your presence to Google Local is properly for an offline store the worst decision you ever made. Adding your site is quite easy:

1.   Go to www.google.com/places

2.   Press "Get your business found on Google"

3.   Sign up and perhaps add Offers (Coupons to attract new customers)

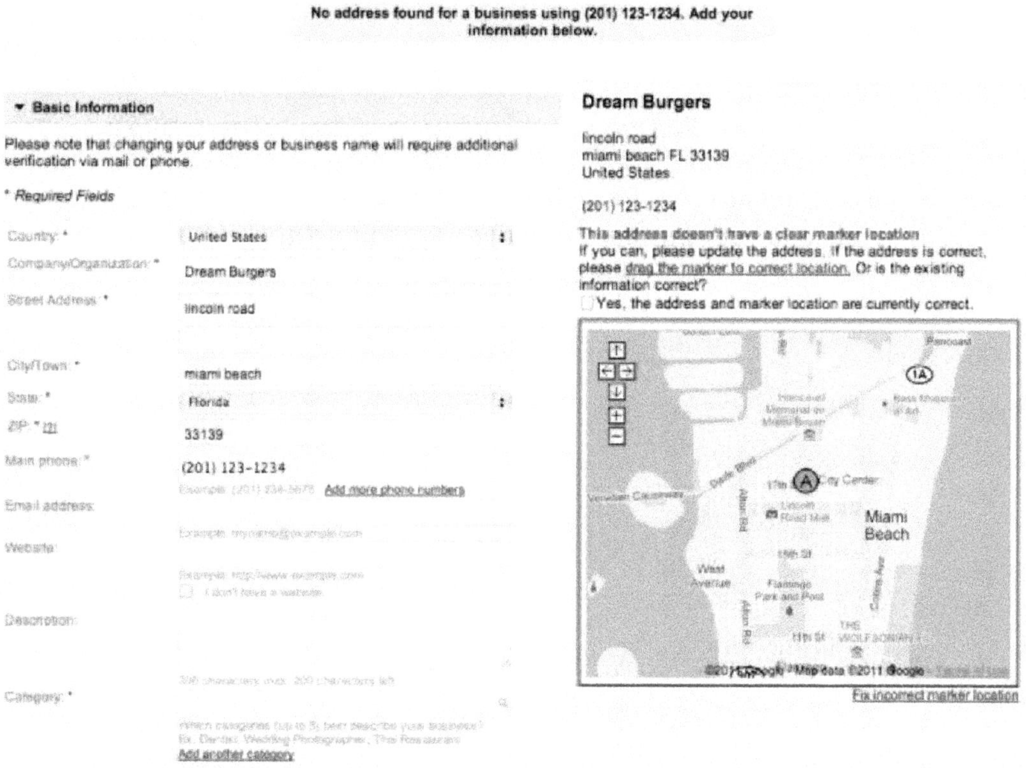

Figure 3.4: Here is an example on how the sign-up screen looks like, and you can add opening hours etc.

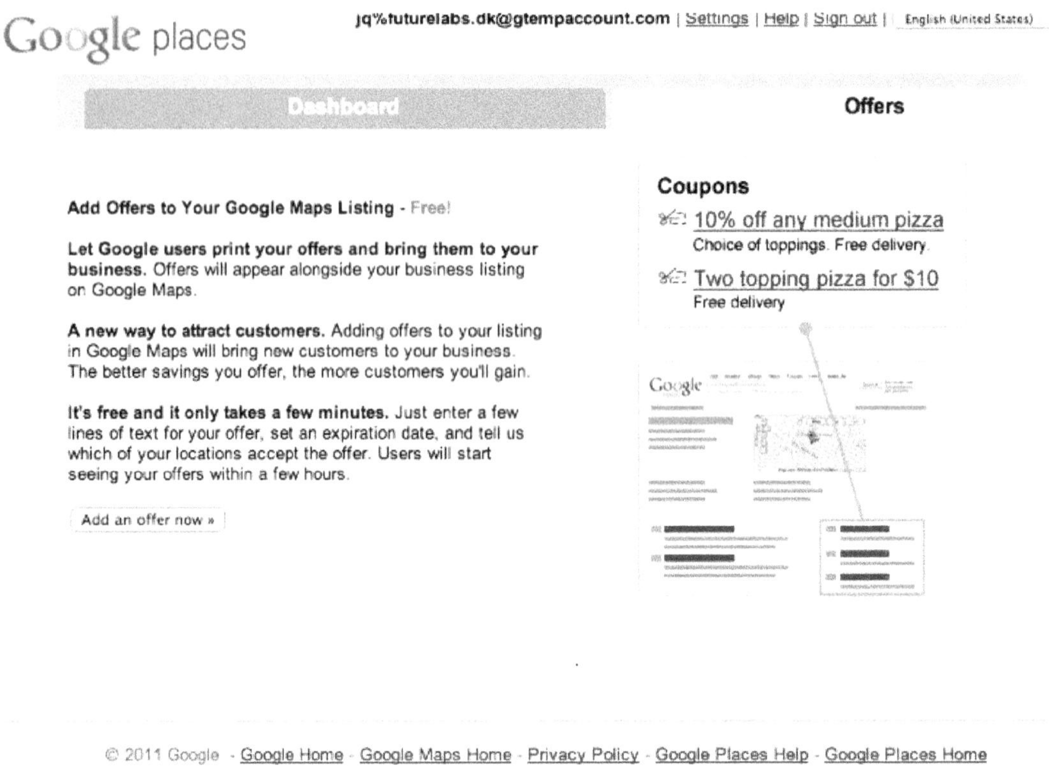
Google places
jq%futurelabs.dk@gtempaccount.com | Settings | Help | Sign out | English (United States)
Dashboard
Offers
Add Offers to Your Google Maps Listing - Free!
Let Google users print your offers and bring them to your business. Offers will appear alongside your business listing on Google Maps.
A new way to attract customers. Adding offers to your listing in Google Maps will bring new customers to your business. The better savings you offer, the more customers you'll gain.
It's free and it only takes a few minutes. Just enter a few lines of text for your offer, set an expiration date, and tell us which of your locations accept the offer. Users will start seeing your offers within a few hours.
Add an offer now »
Coupons
10% off any medium pizza
Choice of toppings. Free delivery.
Two topping pizza for $10
Free delivery
© 2011 Google - Google Home - Google Maps Home - Privacy Policy - Google Places Help - Google Places Home

Figure 3.5: As you can you has the choice to add coupons, which can enhance customers to impulsively to go to your business, and not your competitor!

Enter details of your offer

- Your offer must contain a special discount that is not normally available to customers without an offer.
- Make sure the text is specific, easy to understand and uses good spelling and grammar.
- Check the full Editorial Guidelines for more information.
- Poor quality offers will be removed.

Headline
max. 60 characters

Save 10% with this offer today!

Describe what is on offer and by how much it is discounted.
Example: 15% off any pizza

Details
max. 250 characters

Save 10% on our amazing burgers, but only today!

Describe any terms or restrictions that apply to this offer

Image
(optional)

Add Image

Good until date
max. Oct 31, 2012

Nov 30, 2011

Offer code
(optional)
max. 15 characters

22811245

Distribution ☑ Mobile Phones (learn more)
                  ✓ Printable

At what locations is this offer valid?
◉ All my business locations (3)
○ Choose locations

Before submitting, check the following:

- Does the headline describe a specific offer?
- Are there spelling and grammar errors?
- Do you have permission to use the attached image?

[Cancel] [Publish]

Preview

This is how your offer will look when a customer redeems it at your business.

Printed

Google

[Your business location]
Save 10% with this offer today!

Save 10% on our amazing burgers, but only today!

Code - 22811245   Expires - Nov 30, 2011

Mobile

Show this offer on your phone at the participating business.

Save 10% with this offer today!
[Your business location]
Save 10% on our amazing burgers, but only today!

Code - **22811245**
Expires - **Nov 30, 2011**

This is how your offer will look on your Google maps listing.

Summary

✂ Save 10% with this offer today!
Save 10% on our amazing burgers, but only today!
Expires - Nov 30, 2011

Figure 3.6: As you can you has the choice to add coupons, which can enhance customers to impulsively to go to your business, and not your competitor!

Optimization of Video's

Optimization of video is important like any other media files and YouTube is a great example and by far the most effective video publishing tool when we talk SEO. Remember the quality of your video matters, since the higher quality often brings the views up, and with a higher number of views on YouTube the more relevant is your video for Google. Think about making your video in 3-4 parts if the video is 20 minutes or so. The reason is simply that you got 4 videos that Google will index with your company name product etc. in it, which will heighten your awareness. Here are some basics that you should keep in mind:

- Make a still picture that captures the eye, when you see the picture of a video on YouTube the eye often catches the ones with the best still pictures.
- Look into YouTube for competitors videos with high ranking, the reason why is that you can copy their tags and use it to advance your placement on YouTube on Google (different than regularly SEO).
- Upload your video to a variety of video sites like YouTube, Vimeo etc.
- Use your logo in the video and website address, so people can find you after watching the video.
- Sometimes use the word video or movie in the file name
- If you add the video on your site make sure to write Meta Tags in HTML for the video!
- Go to Fiverr.com and buy views of the video!

Did you learn the following?

☐ Do you understand how a search engine ranks your content?

☐ Did you know that every page is a landing page?

☐ Do you understand how to use headers?

☐ Do you understand how you optimize media files?

☐ You signed up for Google Local?

Own Notes:

_____

_____

_____

_____

_____

_____

_____

_____

CHAPTER

5

"Wikipedia has a world-class link structure (hint! that is why their ranking is so good!)"

5:// **Optimization of links!**

This chapter is all about what is links, why is links so important for your search engine optimization. This chapter is the containing what is in the top of the SEO pyramid. Link building internally and externally is what matters the most in SEO and regardless of your strategy, without the right link building and the right structure will your efforts fail. Look at Wikipedia they are a class act in the online industry, using internal links more frequently than anyone else. Think about it for a moment, why do you think they are number one on Google on about almost any topic you Google? (HINT Their internal and incoming links is what makes the difference!)

Link-Popularity

Link Popularity is among the main factors for search engines when they start to rank your site against competitors. Let's take an example of you and your competitor, both of you sell Cruises to Bahamas and have done exactly the same in the content, meta-tags, optimization of media etc. What site should Google rank highest that's the good questions many could ask? - This is why Link Popularity becomes so important for your website. Google will in that case rank the site with the best link-popularity the highest. Google uses two main parameters to rank the link popularity:

* Number of incoming links (link counts).
* The quality of incoming links (link reputation).

The thing about incoming links is considered a vote on you so if you had a presidential election the obvious is that the guy with the most votes' wins, and that is the same in SEO. The more votes or incoming links you have they better is your popularity and thereby your ranking - the essence in SEO!

The anatomy of a link

Remember that standard HTML, which is the basic for all websites is a link structured around the address and the description that people see about the link. The basic structure is:

<a href="http://www.DOMAIN.com/Cruise-Bahamas/">Cruise to Bahamas</a>

the href is that real webpage url that the user will get to, and what comes after is what they see on the webpage in reality.

Having a file structure in the domain name as mentioned above, is extremely im
portant when Google would index your site, since it will rank it higher than a site
with an url looking like this: www.domain.com/index.php?=id26.

Internal Links:

Having the correct setup for internal links really matters, since it makes it easier
for your visitors and the search engine to navigate on your website. The process is
quite simple, all you have to do is to use descriptive words on each link, that might
seem more relevant for all parts in the process. For example lets say your text and
url is the following: "Dreaming about beaches and vacation? Book your Bahamas
Cruise today!" Since you added the Bahamas in the link will that become part of the
search engine ranking and heighten your chances for a good position. Mouseover
effect is the second part of internal link optimization. What you need is to use the
function called "Title" in the HTML code for your url. This title is the popup
description for a link, when you do your mouse over it, is the same process as with
images. The reason why is that you might want to give the search engine some
information about the specific link and as well the reader who is holding their
mouse over the link, but haven't clicked yet. The codes would as follow in HTML:

- Dreaming about beaches and vacation? Book your
  <a href="http://www.YourWebsite.com/bahamas-cruise/">Bahamas Cruise
  today!"</a>
- Dreaming about beaches and vacation? Book your
  <a href=http://www.YourWebsite.com/bahamas-cruise/" title"This text will
  show on mouse over">Bahamas Cruise today!"</a>

Many websites are using internal linking on their website, but one of the reasons
that Wikipedia have become as successful as they have today, is in fact that internal
link structure is world class.

They have internal links on all content/texts that you read and they are all very descriptive, and this is one of the secrets behind the SEO aspects of Wikipedia, which is far superior.

Figure 3.7: Notice the amount of different descriptive links that Wikipedia uses in the text.

Here are a couple of advices you should consider:

- Think about hos Wikipedia take advantage of internal links in the articles, that is one of their best kept secrets don't use the type of link saying click here.

- Rumors and research shows that unique text with unique link descriptions, often get the best search engine ranking, since you end not competing with anyone else.

- The first unique link on a site is the one that counts the most, so beware of the importance of your links internally.

- Many companies avoid, forget or simply do not know about the secret for internal links, take advantage of it!

- Always remember to have your site name in the URL like www.yoursite.com/**bahamas-cruise**/

Linking to external sites

Linking to other sites has two effects for you, first it needs to create value for your user/customer to click on the link and secondly if the site is respected and relevant Google will rank you higher as well. Google is using the term called Authority sites, which is your gatekeeper and great for newly started websites who wishes to establish their credit on Google. But linking to random sites is not the key to a better ranking, it actually has to be related to the content that you are posting on your site which is great, since people otherwise would have done what Google calls "Black Hat" spamming. What Black Hat is what spammers often do, which is only to increase their ranking (often spammers) by spamming and Google have build mechanisms to eliminate and punish sites doing so. So building external links on your site is the same principle as Wikipedia, you need to have it blended with your content, so the dynamics seems real and right for both the user and Google.

Think about our Cruises to Bahamas again, if you link to an external site from your content about cruises to Bahamas, it might be relevant for the user to read about excursions in Bahamas and it could be a partner that you make money from when they actually go to the external site.

Here are some examples of best practice:

- Only link to external pages, which have content that are relevant for your users.

- Be careful linking to sites that might be spamming the Internet, this will hurt your ranking (link to trusted sites!).

- Always use the setting "blank" meaning that the site will open on a new page, this way the users will always be able to go back to your page.

- If you cannot find a relevant site to link to, they simply don't!

- Remember new user your search keywords describing external links, then you end up telling Google that another site is more important than you!

Keyword Cannibalism

Keyword Cannibalism is pretty simple, you have 2 or more pages fighting for the same ranking, since they use the same parameters for the best ranking. For example you might have one page called cruise and another called cruise Bahamas both words would fight for the same rank on the word cruise. The higher density of related keywords that your website uses, the harder it is to control which sites get the best ranking. Fighting it is easier that you might think here is some best practice examples:

- Never use the same title. If you use different title for your pages, you will simply avoid the first step of keyword cannibalism.

- Optimize for different keywords. Try to use synonyms while optimizing individual posts and avoid confusing the search engines with recurring custom permalink structure.

- Never Over Optimize. People tend to do this a lot of the times and as a result end up ranking a lot of the unwanted posts higher than the required post. So, never over optimize with thematic anchor text links etc.

- Diversify Your Blogs Keywords. While it is advisable to stick to a niche it is not a wise move to use the same keywords all over again and again in all the posts you publish. You might want to use keywords your primary keywords in an attempt to rank high. Use synonyms and some diversity and this will not only keep your blog from keyword cannibalism but also keep your readers interested. Remember – Variety is often very good!
- Uses of "words" would eliminate it to a certain extend.

Incoming links are gold!

Think about incoming links for a moment, I kept writing in the past chapters that these are more significant in your ranking than any other parameter. If we Google the search word laptop you will find at this point Apple to be number 5 on the list, and if you pay attention the search word laptop do not exist on their website. It does not exist in the Content, Title or Meta description. So that leads us all to an important questions, how did they manage to rank number 5 on such a heavy search keyword, with one of the highest densities on the market? The answer is quite simple, people are linking to Apple's website, and this way they are able to obtain this unique position. This is a great example of the importance of incoming links and why they are gold!

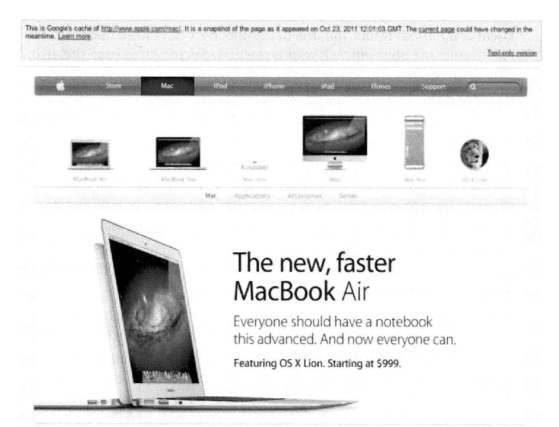

Figure 3.8: shows that apple in the cached version does not contain the word Laptop.

Here is a list of great examples on how you can build great links which is convertible like gold!!!

- **People love lists.** Build some list like a "101 ways to cruise" people love to link to these (Hint, Hint). Top 10-myth article about your topic. Include a list of experts of Gurus, which people would link to.

- **Developing Authority & Being Easy to Link to**. Make your content easy to understand, eliminate spelling mistakes.

- **Pay Per Click**. Buy relevant traffic from Google and other sites.

- **News & Syndication**. Use pages like EzineArticles.com, GoArticles.com for syndication and traffic. Send out a press release with services like Pressking.com. Trade articles with other webmasters.

- **Local & Business Links**. Join the Better Business Bureau so that they would link to your site bbb.com. Ask your trade partners to link to your site. Use affiliate programs.

- **Use free links**. Use of Craigslist, Yahoo! Answers, Google Groups, Wikipedia are among the tools that are free if relevant and you can easily start building up a ranking here.

- **Love people who review your site or product**. Make sure that you get as many points of your reviews (customers) on pages like Amazon.com.

- **Blog!** Create a blog and link back to your site could help as well, and if someone likes your blog post and syndicate it, then you are right on track!

- **Buy an established site.** Sometimes it make sense to buy sites with a high SEO ranking, just to use them for link building if the owner of the site do not realize the real value of the site.

- **Giveaways**. People love to tell their friends about something free and blog posters like to advertise it to entertain and give their audience something.

- **Get Sued**. Think about suing a big corporation you might end up in practically all newspaper and online resources that are trusted, talk about link building in no time!

Beware of some links!

Think about the real world, a recommendation from a good friend might influence you to buy, but if you get the recommendation from someone whom you do not trust, you might think no I it will buy else where or something else. Well Google, Bing and Yahoo! does their business in their algorithms the same way. They rank websites and if you have a high rank of blacklisted sites linked to you, this might influence your ranking to a huge extend. Think about this, you could harm your competition by finding hackers, using specific sites ranking a competition down this are known as link farms. This might not be legal but in your ears it might sound appealing. Well be careful to monitor if you have links like these linking in, and ask your webhost to block their IP to eliminate their server counting towards your site.

Use Google Analytics and other Google products to monitor your site, and if someone clicks on a link, linking into your site you would be able to know it. Luckily here is a list of thins you should not do!

- **Avoid directories**. There is a bunch of sites selling you link building that just post you to directories, these do nothing for you other than wasting money!

- **Spam other sites and forums**. Spamming other sites with your link it not a good practice and Google look at is as a black hat SEO technique.

- **Garbage link exchanges.** Send link exchange emails, which look like an automated bot sent them (little or no customization, no personal names, etc.).

- **Being a jerk**. No one wants to do business with a jerk, and spamming others, stealing content etc. does not help, it only give you problems!

- **Monitor your site.** Use Google Webmaster tool and Google Alerts to monitor your website and know if someone is harming your position.

Who is linking to your website?

Finding out who is linking to your website might be easier than you thought of, luckily does all the search engines have tools to monetize it for you. It is always healthy and good to know for your own knowledge who and how many is linking, if the number rises without any particular reason like a product launch you might start to wonder why?

Here is a list of ways that you can obtain the knowledge about who are linking to you:

- Majesticseo.com is selling a membership that monitors the density on your website and explains how your density is compared to competitors.

- Open Site Explorer is another great tool, which is offered by SEOmoz, which can be accessed on opensiteexplorer.org, and it allows you to obtain basically all data you need.

- Yahoo Site Explorer is free and offered by Yahoo and can be accessed by clicking onto http://siteexplorer.search.yahoo.com

Figure 3.9: Example of MajesticSEO for Norwegian Cruise line.

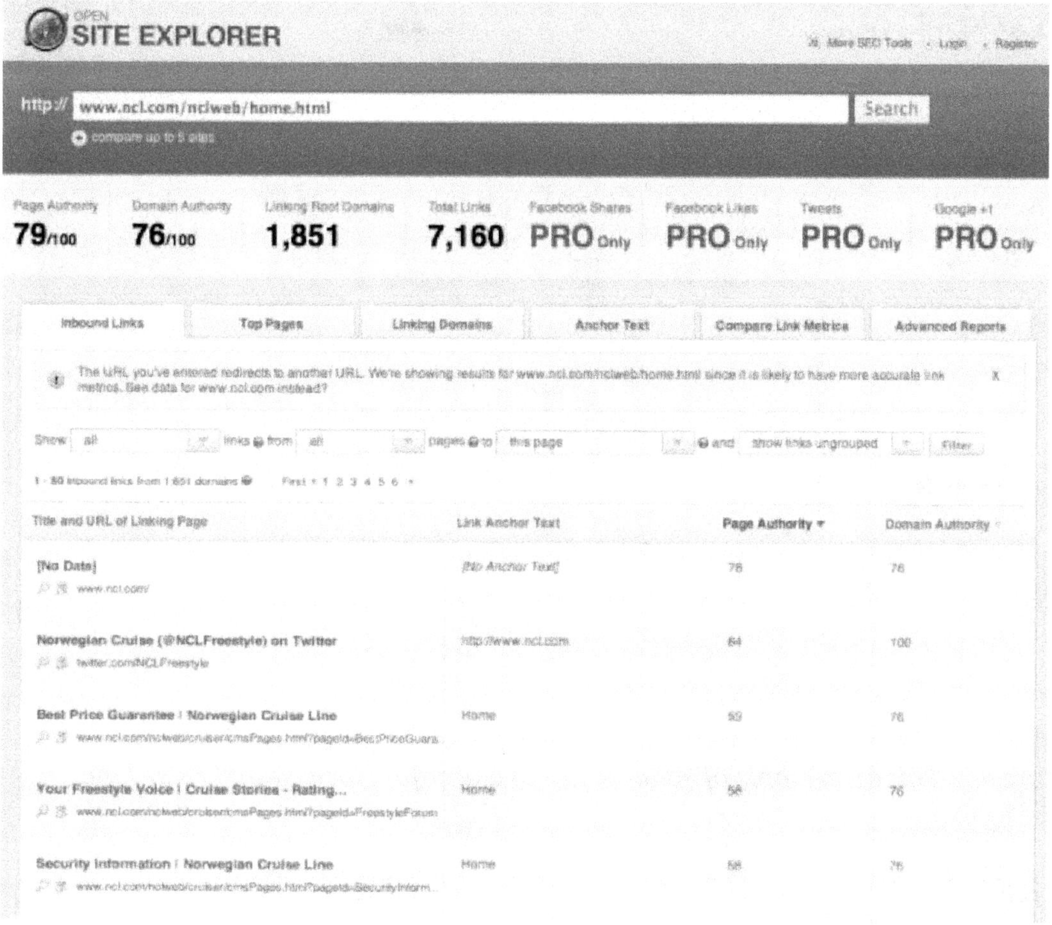

Figure 4.1: Example of Open Site Explorer for Norwegian Cruise line.

Figure 4.2: This an example of Yahoo's Site Explorer for Norwegian Cruise Line.

Make it easy to share your content

Social media integration is more important and popular than ever, and honestly it does not hurt when customers endorse your products or services to their social surroundings on Facebook, Twitter, Google+ etc. Making it easy to do so is your job, and if you fail to do so, you will not only miss out on a great opportunity but also a possibility to get a better ranking on Google, Bing and Yahoo. The best way to make sharing right and easy is to do the following:

- Implement a product like addthis.com or simple just go to https://developers.facebook.com/docs/reference/plugins/like/ , http://twitter.com/about/resources/tweetbutton and http://www.google.com/+1/button/ these are the 3 mostly common used sharing sites and then LinkedIn is another example for a fourth one.

- Use a descriptive URL in the share like www.yourdomain.com/Cruise-Bahamas so you gain advantage in SEO.

- Insert a Book my page button on your website.

- Add a Tip a friend or share with a friend button, very common on news sites.

Publish a press release

Releasing a press release might be something your organization does frequently or rarely. When you publish a press release it might pay of to think about SEO again, since this is a part your SEO universe and it most likely would benefit your ranking. Remember if you use services such as Pressking, Presswire etc. to publish your press release with it would pay of to add internal links or at least in the fact box for the article, this way would you end up linking back and guides the possible reader to your site.

Here are some examples of what you should consider:

- Find the keywords that relates to your story and use those as a part of it.

- Insert some links to your own website that are factual and proves your point showcases what you are writing about.

- Optimize the keywords as you learned in chapter 4.

- Do not use more than two links to your own website (since if there are more it could be considered spam).

- Don't let the links link to the same site on your website (use different URL'S).

- Publish your press releases on different platforms and see what works best for you!

- Do not over optimize since the reader would miss the point, engage them at first!

Social Media and link building

Think about your own use of Social Media today, you might click on more recommendation's from friends today since they wrote it on their Twitter, LinkedIn or Facebook update. Social Media linking is considered a non-follow tag from Google meaning that they do give you a significant value in terms of ranking. But they give you a different value, word-of-mouth is properly the most significant advantage that you might get, and then search engine ranking looks at the following factors when indexing from social medias:

- When someone recommend you on social medias, and their friends start doing the same you will end up seeing a viral effect where your impact goes up and people link to your on third-party sites giving you an advantage!

- Your domain popularity is the only part that will go up in terms of SEO when you gain awareness in social media. The domain popularity tells Google how trusted your site is, and it the effect is small but still better than not having any effect. Remember Google might change their Algorithm in the future, since social media is gaining a higher and higher importance! The algorithm from Google looks into the following when ranking your site from social medias.

- Number of followers on Twitter.

- Number of Tweets and re-tweets.

- Number of fans on your Facebook fan page.

- The sharing rate on Facebook of your links and fan page.

- The authority of the people that follow you on Twitter.

- Number of unique mentions (like @jqvist).

- Ratio on Twitter followers/following.

Ideas for you to initiate!

Remember developing your site, awareness and responsiveness towards your customers are the key to success in today's competitive environment. If your market is global or local there are thousands of ways to capture new customers without investing too much $$$$ in advertising. Here is some examples of things that you should consider in order to gain your SEO ranking and actually do something unique for your brand, awareness and being different than the rest!

- **A picture says more than 1,000 words**. Remember info graphics the small teasers that the Tech-blogs loves to publish? – Well they are extremely informative and people love to share them, this will increase not only your awareness but also your business!

- **Share your knowledge**. Sharing your knowledge on social media channels is a great way to engage your followers, so they get something out of being loyal to your company. If you shave something unique you can be sure that they will tell their friends as well!

- **Blogging**. People like to follow interesting blogs that get updated once in a while and this also improves your SEO ranking if you use internal links in the blog posts.

- **Customer service**. Do I need to mention Zappo's? – Well they are notoriously famous for their customer service and that is the key to their success. (Imagine the free press exposure they got!!!)

- **Livestream of video content**. If your company does a lot of events it might payoff to livestream these online using Ustream.com to show your customers. Maybe make webinars and showcase your business. Do you have a factory well most people like to spend time seeing how things are build, and if you make a video believe it could go viral = $$$$$ in increased sales.

- **Sharing with social media.** Leaving out the sharing buttons as described in this chapter would be like taking your car on a trip for 100 miles even though you only have gasoline for 30 miles. This is a must, people like to care and show others what they like etc.

Did you learn the following?

☐ Did you learn what link popularity means and how it works in practice?

☐ Do you understand keyword cannibalism?

☐ You know who links to your website?

☐ Do you understand the difference between internal and external links?

☐ Do you understand how important incoming linking is? (I.E. Laptop, Apple)

☐ You got an understanding how to optimize your content in terms of links?

Own Notes:

_____

_____

_____

_____

_____

_____

_____

_____

CHAPTER

6

"There are many ways you can end up harming your SEO efforts more than you do good!"

6:// Techniques that will harm your SEO ranking!

I have been talking on and off about Black Hat SEO in this book and it might have confused you, but it is extremely important that you know the terminology and how to avoid falling into the traps. You obviously have a great business or thinking about creating one. The problem is if you engage in Black Hat SEO you might harm your business to such an extend, that Google first of all will blacklist you and it will take forever to gain a reasonable ranking again. Remember that Google, Bing, Yahoo!, Yandex (Russia), Baidu (China) are the biggest virtual market places in the world by far and it hurts to be left out from them! This chapter is made for you so you avoid the common mistakes, and you stay ahead and in the game!

The Search engines are Kings!

You should always know the rules and regulations and guidelines that the search engines have posted, since you would like to know what they do not want you to do period! Unfortunately are they are the kings of the online world at this point, while social media is moving closer and closer into this market place. The sole problem is that you must act the way that they want you too otherwise it is game over! The problem is that in fact a lot of people think about SEO as, how can I trick the search engine to a better position, well you could do so in the 1990's, but today that is considered Black Hat SEO to do so. The search engines knows that people watch out for others, which is why you can actually turn in your competitor for spam if they do so. Google want you to be a watchdog for others and they take that part seriously. If Google were filled with spam no one would ever use it's service if you keep that in mind.

You can turn in a competitor on www.google.com/contact/spamreport.html and if you do the slightest black hat SEO you can be sure a competitor would turn you in!

Google's Guidelines for Webmasters:

Following these guidelines will help Google find, index, and rank your site. Even if you choose not to implement any of these suggestions, we strongly encourage you to pay very close attention to the "Quality Guidelines," which outline some of the illicit practices that may lead to a site being removed entirely from the Google index or otherwise impacted by an algorithmic or manual spam action. If a site has been affected by a spam action, it may no longer show up in results on Google.com or on any of Google's partner sites.

When your site is ready:

- Submit it to Google at http://www.google.com/addurl.html.

- Submit a Sitemap using Google Webmaster Tools. Google uses your Sitemap to learn about the structure of your site and to increase our coverage of your webpages.

- Make sure all the sites that should know about your pages are aware your site is online.

Design and content guidelines:

- Make a site with a clear hierarchy and text links. Every page should be reachable from at least one static text link.

- Offer a site map to your users with links that point to the important parts of your site. If the site map has an extremely large number of links, you may want to break the site map into multiple pages.

- Keep the links on a given page to a reasonable number.

- Create a useful, information-rich site, and write pages that clearly and accurately describe your content.

- Think about the words users would type to find your pages, and make sure that your site actually includes those words within it.

- Try to use text instead of images to display important names, content, or links. The Google crawler doesn't recognize text contained in images. If you must use images for textual content, consider using the "ALT" attribute to include a few words of descriptive text.

- Make sure that your <title> elements and ALT attributes are descriptive and accurate.

- Check for broken links and correct HTML.

- If you decide to use dynamic pages (i.e., the URL contains a "?" character), be aware that not every search engine spider crawls dynamic pages as well as static pages. It helps to keep the parameters short and the number of them few.

- Review our recommended best practices for images and video. (find it on their website)

Technical guidelines:

- Use a text browser such as Lynx to examine your site, because most search engine spiders see your site much as Lynx would. If fancy features such as JavaScript, cookies, session IDs, frames, DHTML, or Flash keep you from seeing all of your site in a text browser, then search engine spiders may have trouble crawling your site.

- Allow search bots to crawl your sites without session IDs or arguments that track their path through the site. These techniques are useful for tracking individual user behavior, but the access pattern of bots is entirely different. Using these techniques may result in incomplete indexing of your site, as bots may not be able to eliminate URLs that look different but actually point to the same page.

- Make sure your web server supports the If-Modified-Since HTTP header. This feature allows your web server to tell Google whether your content has changed since we last crawled your site. Supporting this feature saves you bandwidth and overhead.

- Make use of the robots.txt file on your web server. This file tells crawlers which directories can or cannot be crawled. Make sure it's current for your site so that you don't accidentally block the Googlebot crawler. Visit http://www.robotstxt.org/faq.html to learn how to instruct robots when they visit your site. You can test your robots.txt file to make sure you're using it correctly with the robots.txt analysis tool available in Google Webmaster Tools.

- Make reasonable efforts to ensure that advertisements do not affect search engine rankings. For example, Google's AdSense ads and DoubleClick links are blocked from being crawled by a robots.txt file.

- If your company buys a content management system, make sure that the system creates pages and links that search engines can crawl.

- Use robots.txt to prevent crawling of search results pages or other auto-generated pages that don't add much value for users coming from search engines.

- Test your site to make sure that it appears correctly in different browsers.

- Monitor your site's performance and optimize load times. Google's goal is to provide users with the most relevant results and a great user experience. Fast sites increase user satisfaction and improve the overall quality of the web (especially for those users with slow Internet connections), and we hope that as webmasters improve their sites, the overall speed of the web will improve. Google strongly recommends that all webmasters regularly monitor site performance using Page Speed, YSlow, WebPagetest, or other tools. For more information, tools, and resources, see Let's Make The Web Faster. In addition, the Site Performance tool in Webmaster Tools shows the speed of your website as experienced by users around the world.

Quality guidelines:

These quality guidelines cover the most common forms of deceptive or manipulative behavior, but Google may respond negatively to other misleading practices not listed here (e.g. tricking users by registering misspellings of well-known websites). It's not safe to assume that just because a specific deceptive technique isn't included on this page, Google approves of it. Webmasters who spend their energies upholding the spirit of the basic principles will provide a much better user experience and subsequently enjoy better ranking than those who spend their time looking for loopholes they can exploit.

If you believe that another site is abusing Google's quality guidelines, please report that site at https://www.google.com/webmasters/tools/spamreport. Google prefers developing scalable and automated solutions to problems, so we attempt to minimize hand-to-hand spam fighting. The spam reports we receive are used to create scalable algorithms that recognize and block future spam attempts.

Quality guidelines - basic principles:

- Make pages primarily for users, not for search engines. Don't deceive your users or present different content to search engines than you display to users, which is commonly referred to as "cloaking."

- Avoid tricks intended to improve search engine rankings. A good rule of thumb is whether you'd feel comfortable explaining what you've done to a website that competes with you. Another useful test is to ask, "Does this help my users? Would I do this if search engines didn't exist?"

- Don't participate in link schemes designed to increase your site's ranking or PageRank. In particular, avoid links to web spammers or "bad neighbor hoods" on the web, as your own ranking may be affected adversely by those links.

- Don't use unauthorized computer programs to submit pages, check rankings, etc. Such programs consume computing resources and violate our Terms of Service. Google does not recommend the use of products such as WebPosition Gold™ that send automatic or programmatic queries to Google.

Quality guidelines - specific guidelines:
- Avoid hidden text or hidden links.
- Don't use cloaking or sneaky redirects.
- Don't send automated queries to Google.
- Don't load pages with irrelevant keywords.
- Don't create multiple pages, subdomains, or domains with substantially duplicate content.
- Don't create pages with malicious behavior, such as phishing or installing viruses, trojans, or other badware.
- Avoid "doorway" pages created just for search engines, or other "cookie cutter" approaches such as affiliate programs with little or no original content.
- If your site participates in an affiliate program, make sure that your site adds value. Provide unique and relevant content that gives users a reason to visit your site first.

If you determine that your site doesn't meet these guidelines, you can modify your site so that it does and then submit your site for reconsideration.

How to Avoid Black Hat SEO:

Think about the Google guidelines if you do not follow those, you are considered to do what is Black Hat SEO. To make it easier for you to understand, is this list concluded for you so you know what you should avoid, and writing it down, taking a copy to hang it up or simply open the book on this page would be extremely valuable for you on a daily basis if you do web development.

Invisible links:

Invisible links is links that are in the HTML code, but your customers cannot see it with their eyes. The reason why this happens is often that if you do a link exchange with another company, you might want to keep it on your site, but you change the link color to the same as the background so it become invisible, the reasons are that you will keep it for SEO reasons, but you actually end up making the search engine think you are cheating for a better ranking!

Invisible Text:

Spammers will often have some text written in white on a white background, this might seem smart, since you suddenly have content on your website that seems to enhance your keywords. The only problem is that search engines can read your code and they see this as a site that whishes to spam.

Tiny text

Spammers often bomb a site with small text in the bottom of their page since they want important search words to reflect their site. Often this text is written so small that the regular people cannot even read the text. Sometimes people use invisible text, which as the links have the same background.

Keyword spam

If you spam your Meta-Description, Title-Tags and Meta-Keywords settings on your website with too many keywords, the search engines would see it as an attempt to cheat. Don't try to be a jack-of-all-trade rather focuses on something different. A friend of mine once told me I went in to one of the most online competitive business you can image. I decided to take a niche approach changing my keywords and turn it upside down, otherwise I would have ended up fighting for the same space (which I couldn't afford) and that way he ended up as one of the biggest players in the market.

Link farms

Avoid for any costs to buy link placements from a link farm, search engines spot them right away and you end up wasting money and time. It might be great in the short run, but you loose control of your incoming links and could end up hurting more than you are doing good.

Splogs

Spamming + Blogs = Splogs, often companies tend to hire cheap SEO "experts" form Asia, and they will post you site as spam on Blogs all over the place, and believe me on my own blog it happens about a couple hundred times a day. The good thing is that search engines became better at capturing this way of doing link building, and if you do it to a certain extend, you are black listed!

Doorway Pages & Cloaking

It is a very sophisticated method to cheat the search engines, what simply happens is that you create a site targeted for the search engines when they crawl that your users never sees. This site is obviously created to enhance your ranking, but search engines have learned how to spot sites like these over time, and this is another example of what not to do!

Scraper Sites

You simple steal the content from sites that already are ranked high on search engines. The process is often atomized and it will post it on different sites targeting link building towards you, only problem is that you will be identified at some point.

Too much optimization

If you do too much search engine optimization you will trick the search engine to think that you started to spam people, and your agenda for the day is not proper. The problem is that you might end up being deleted from the search engine rankings, since they would find your site too "perfect" for it's category.

No ownership of your SEO efforts

A huge variety of companies will try to sell you subscription to SEO services, this is very nice in the start but if you stop paying, you will loose all the work they have done. This is a very strategic move, which leads you to a question?

- Do you want to lock-in to a supplier the rest of your business life?
- Plus you never know if they do changes that actually would hurt your ranking.

Did you learn the following?

☐ Do you know Google's Policy for webmasters?
☐ Do you understand what Black Hat SEO is?
☐ Do You know what to do to avoid Black Hat SEO?

Own Notes:

_____

_____

_____

_____

_____

_____

_____

_____

_____

CHAPTER

7

"Did you know a good page strucutre matters, and it's often free to adapt a system for that?"

7:// **Optimize your page structure**

Think about it for a second, you got the perfect designed website as you wanted it to be, but did you keep SEO in mind in the process? – Your great design might not be very SEO friendly and that would leave out important visitors for you. Having a search friendly site is alpha-omega in today's business world, and that is something you need to keep in mind! It does not cost much to have a professional to check your website, in fact www.futurelabs.dk a Danish domain but an agency out of Miami would be able to assist you in your needs and they are very fair in their pricing.

Basic principles to remember

Remember your URL structure is important and having the right Content Management System (CMS), Blog system, E-commerce solution would be at high importance for you, since these have build in SEO efforts and follow the page structure and guides you when you build your website, and makes it easier to maintain in the long run. Headers have to be in the right order as you learned earlier in this book and those are things that you need to be aware of. Remember that you can by using Google's Webmaster tool www.google.com/webmasters/tools you would be able to see how Google is perceiving your website.

Picking the right CMS, Blog or Ecommerce system

Picking the right CMS, Blog or Ecommerce system is not only concerning SEO but it also makes it easier to maintain a website in the long run, if you invest in the right system (Hint the best ones are FREE)! If you want a basic website would systems like Joomla, Wordpress and Drupal often beat the best and system and with www.themeforest.net you can actually buy basic designs to add on for a price range of $35-90 for a pre-made design structure. Investing in the right platform if you do some research is actually cheaper than you might have thought of! If you use the right platform you might be able due to increased SEO performance to increase your visitor base with 50-100% in many cases! Here is a list of great systems that all are free or very cheap:

Blogs:

- **Wordpress** - the most widely used system on the web www.wordpress.org
- **Tumblr** - the upcoming blog system, that is growing like a rocket, the benefit with Tumblr is that it is easy to integrate and it is hosted in the cloud and free www.tumblr.com

Ecommerce:

- **Magento** – is the most advanced ecommerce system available today there is a free version and premium versions www.magento.com

- **Shopify** – is a new simple cloud hosted system that is extremely simple to use for anyone that wishes to open a ecommerce store www.shopify.com

- **OsCommerce** – one of the most widely used systems on the internet www.oscommerce.com

CMS:

- **Joomla** – is very simple and the platform that has the highest popularity, open source and a huge amount of updates and themes available www.joomla.org

- **Drupal** – is number two in the CMS systems that are based on open source and another example of a simple but yet advanced system available www.drupal.org

- **Expressionengine** – Is the easiest of the mentioned CMS systems for a new comer to start of with (but you pay for it!) www.expressionengine.com

What all these sites have in common is the fact that they all are optimized for SEO, and that is why you should consider using systems like these for your web development.

Does your website support W3C?

W3C is an online standard today, and it is important for performance, how the search engine reads your site that you are optimized by W3C standards. The reasons as you might guess are many, you want your site to be ranked high (without the right coding forget it!), the load time for the user is less etc. here are some example of why you want to optimize!:

- Mobile phones are optimized by W3C and this allows your site to be loaded faster on a mobile device, and you do not wish to leave out that segment due to bad optimization and page load, do you?

- You website would be compatible in all browsers (Internet Explorer, Safari, Firefox, Chrome and Opera).

- Think about asking your developer to follow the W3C standards, this would eventually leave out the basic mistakes he might create on the other hand.

It is easy to check if your website is optimized according to the consortium behind the standard do they offer a free tool to evaluate your website. The tool can be accesses on http://validator.W3.org all you have to do is to insert the URL you wish to test and then you would see a result like this:

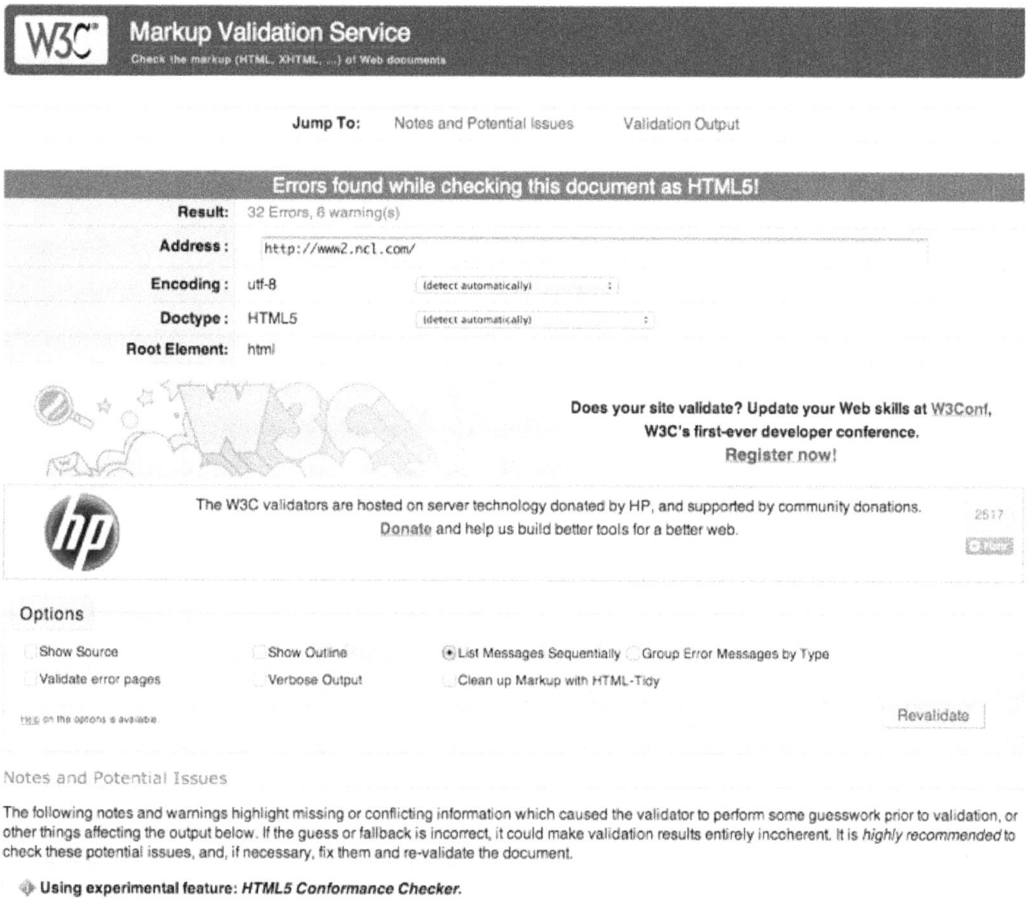

Figure: 4.3: W3C illustration

As you can see Norwegian Cruise Line has 32 errors they need to work on and 6 issues that needs to be fixed right away (BTW if you scroll down, the site will show you what is wrong). Here is an illustration of some of the mistakes that NCL should ask their developers to fix:

Figure: 4.4: What you would need to correct in order to comply with W3C!

Always use text instead of images (if possible)

As I explained in chapter 4 search engines prefer text, since it is easier to index and showcase for their customers. Images are a great tool and they do say more than 1,000 words so if you decided to use an image remember to optimize it for the search engines so you keep your PageRank. Think about it if you upload a picture of an island in Bahamas, Google would not be able to see that fantastic beach that you are showcasing, it can only "show/read" it if you write it in text. Avoid flash, mobile devices cannot read them in most cases and Google have problems indexing flash. Think about the design process of a website, it is easy just to add images, buttons etc. It all looks amazing and helps your design, BUT if you forget to SEO optimize the graphical elements, you will not only loose points, but Google, Bing and Yahoo! would in cases leave you out of their rankings. What most people don't know is that you can by using HTML, CSS and Graphic would be able to use perfect graphics that the search engines can read and would understand.

Advice: Check how Google reads your website by searching on your site by the following code: "cache:yoursite.com" – after click on the text only version, this way you would be able to see if your site is "Google ready"!

Search keywords in the URL

The use of search keywords in your URL is as mentioned before extremely important and a part of your goals! It is highly important to use the right structure like:

- www.YourSite.com/Bahamas-cruise
- www.YourSite.com/Bahamas-cruise.html
- www.Yoursite.com/index.php?id=7 (this type of URL is a no go!)

Notice sites like Amazon.com uses the above mentioned principles and there are reasons why they do so. As you see all products that Amazon Showcase have their names in the URL, that is purely for SEO purposes, and they know if Amazon.com comes up first when people they Google "A Winner's DNA" they would most likely end up with the sale and make the money.

This is the most widely used advice for URL structure:

- Never use Underscore or space in a URL use a dash like: www.YourSite.com/Bahamas-cruise
- Avoid URL's like this www.Yoursite.com/index.php?id=7 (does not make any sense to any one!)
- Do you sell a specific product, you might want to specify the product group first like: www.YourSite.com/Cruise/Bahamas-cruise
- Don't let the URL become longer than 70 words.
- If you change an URL use the redirect 301 method, otherwise you will loose the existing ranking for that particular page (described later in this chapter).

Figure 4.4: Illustration of Amazon's URL structure

Duplicate Content and how to avoid it

Duplicate content simply means that you have two sites with the same content, and these will both fight for the same SEO ranking. There could be many reasons why you have Duplicate content and some of them are often basic issues on your web site that can be solved easily. Many websites have a print now button which brings you to a page with the same content as you just left, but Google will look at booth of them as "duplicates". It is fairly easy to avoid that Google Index the Print page, by simply doing the following adding a noindex follow tag and a canonical tag:

<link rel="canonical" href="http://www.YOurSite.org/Print/Bahamas-Cruise" />

(This is for the Print Now Link)

<head>

<meta name="robots" content="noindex, follow" />

</head>

By using a noindex, follow method you would avoid having the pages you do not wish to be indexed, indexed on Google. If you do not use the noindex follow method you will start to fight with yourself for rankings, and the search engines look at duplicate content as a minus, so you would loose free points! Duplicate content can also appear when people copy content from your website and start to publish it. You can always monitor if someone copies you, and you might be able to sue them in the case they do so!

- **www.copyscape.com** - is a great product to monitor if someone duplicate your content, so you can stop freeloaders on your behalf (remember they might hurt your ranking by copying you!)

- **Google Alerts** – You can as well use Google Alerts to monitor your site, all you need to do is to add some unique sentences and Google will send you an email if those get crawled up on the net – just go to www.google.com/alerts

Here is an example of how Copyscape captured to copies of content from www.jesperqvist.com (which is my bio so it should come up)

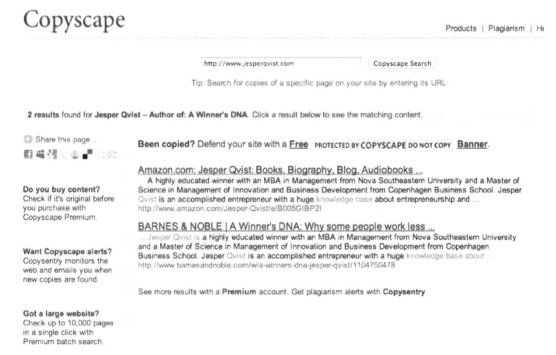

Figure 4.5: How Copyscape captures duplicate content

Google Alerts is simple and you just add a sentence, name etc. – here is an example of Jesper Qvist:

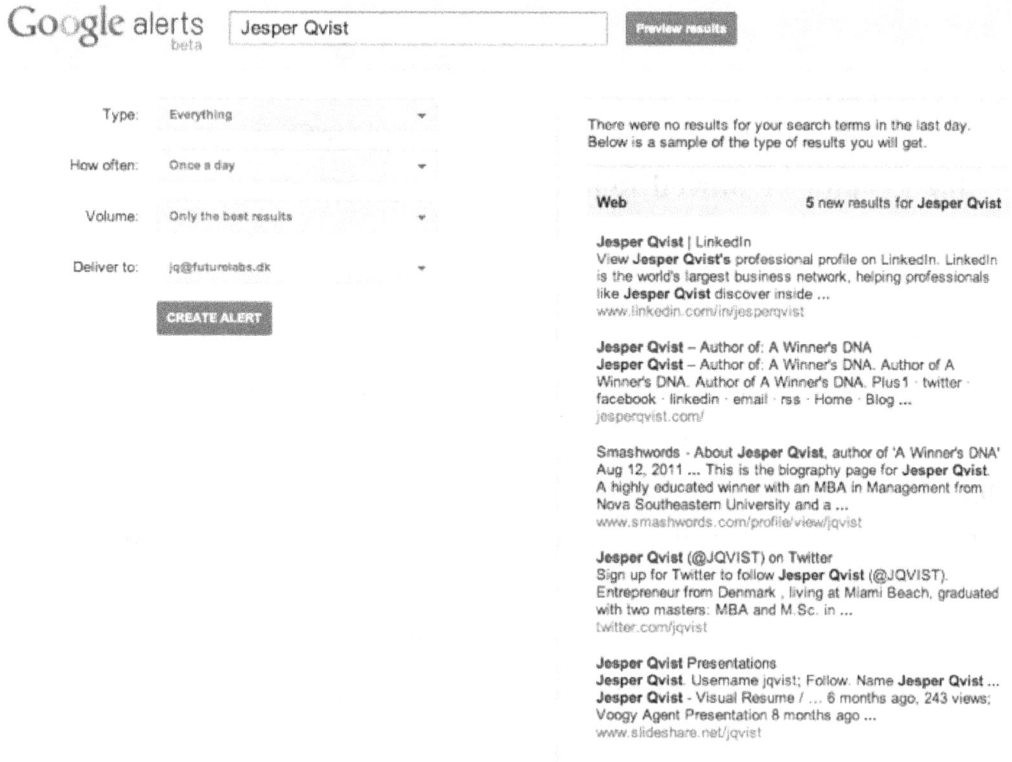

Figure 4.6: Google Alerts for Jesper Qvist

Finally the most common mistakes that people do when Duplicate Content occurs:

- Your URL structures are identical
- Lack of noindex, follow use.
- Print-friendly pages are duplicate content (use noindex, follow)
- Competition would copy your content
- Your domain names have different country codes but showcase the same website like (Apple.com, Apple.co.uk, Apple.de etc.)

- You uploaded documents to your website with identical content as on the website.

Redirect 301 (move a website)

There are three types of Redirects that you need to be aware of:

- **301 ('Moved Permanently')** - Recommended for SEO
- **302 ('Found' or 'Moved Temporarily')**
- **Meta Refresh**

The basics of a redirect are in its simplest form, the process when you send the search engine or user to a different URL than they originally requested. The problem is if you do not use the redirect 301 method you would loose ranking credits. According to a huge quantity of test would a website that uses 301 redirect codes keep 90-99% of the rank credits when redirecting. If you temporarily move a link with redirect 302 and you will not gain any credit for that methods (which is why you should never do so!). Meta Refresh is a different method that you should avoid as well. The best practice for redirects is simply describes as: People type in page A and you direct them to Page B. If you do not use a redirect 301 for that situation would Google have no idea if the page has moved, but since you complied with redirect 301, they will give you credit for your actions. Be aware that when moving a page from one URL to another, the search engines will take some time to discover the redirect 301, time to recognize it, and credit the new page with the rankings and trust it. The pro cess might be longer that you wish for, but there is nothing to do about it. If you consider redirect 302 or Meta refreshes, you should be aware that they are poor sub stitutes, as they generally will not pass the rankings and search engine values like a 301 redirect will. The only time these redirects are good alternatives is if a Webmaster purposefully doesn't want to pass link credit on from the old page to the new!

Redirects can be tricky but here are the most widely used methods:

1. Redirecting specific files and folders from one domain to another:
You need a redirection from the old server to the new one with your filenames preserved.

Example:
Redirect: http://www.YOURDOMAIN.com/cruise/somefile.php To:
http://www.YOURDOMAIN.org/somefile.php

Solution:
Add the following directive to the applicable file on your server:
RedirectMatch 301 /cruise/(.*) http://www.YOURDOMAIN.com/$1

Explanation:
The regular expression /cruise/(.*) tells apache to match the cruise folder followed by zero or more of any characters. Surrounding the .* in parenthesis tells apache to save the matched string as a back-reference. This back-reference is placed at the end of the URL that was directed to, in this case, $1.

2. Redirecting Canonical Hostnames:
You would Canonical Hostnames to avoid common canonicalization errors.
Redirect: http://YourDomain.com/
To: http:// YourDomain.com/
Redirect: http://mail. YourDomain.com/
To: http://www. YourDomain.com
Redirect: http:// YourDomain.com/somefile.php
To: http://www. YourDomain.com/somefile.php

Solution:

Add the following directive:

RewriteCond %{HTTP_HOST} ^YourDomain\.com [NC]

RewriteRule (.*) http://www.YourDomain.com/$1 [L,R=301]

Explanation:

This directive tells apache to examine the host the visitor is accessing (in this case: YourDomain.com), and if it does not equal www.YourDomain.com redirect to www. YourDomain.com. The exclamation point (!) in front of www.YourDomain.com denies the comparison, saying, "if the host IS NOT www.YourDomain.com, then perform RewriteRule." In our case RewriteRule redirects them to www.YourDomain. com while upholding the exact file they were accessing in a back-reference.

3. Redirecting without preserving the filename:

You moved your site and several files that existed on the old server are no longer present on the new server. Instead of maintaining the file names in the redirection (which would result in a Error 404 not found error on the new server), the old files needs to be redirected to the root URL of the new domain.

Redirect: http://www.YourDomain.com/cruise/someoldfile.php

To: http://www.YourDomain.com/

Solution:

Add the following directive:

RedirectMatch 301 /cruise/someoldfile.php http://www.YourDomain.com

Explanation:

Excluding any parenthesis, all requests for /cruise/someoldfile.php should redirect to the root URL of http://www.YourDomain.com

404 Error Pages

Sometimes it happens that websites shows an error message called error 404, which means that the server is either over-loaded, there is a technical malfunction or simply the page that you are trying to access are not redirected properly or de leted. 404 error pages really matter, since they get shown to your customers once in a while. There are some basic rules you should follow when creating a 404-error page:

- Present the user for what's important, your logo, contact information and a link to the FrontPage.
- Provide them with a contact us function.
- Make the layout fit the existing layout of your website, so they feel like they still are with you.
- Don't write ERROR-404, the user might not understand that, write it in a simple way that an error have occurred and you apologies.

If you want to setup an error 404 file it is quite easy, all you need to do is to access the .htaccess-file on your server and add the following line:

- ErrorDocument 4040 http://www.YourDomain.com/404.html

On the next page will you find a funny example of a good Error-404 page:

134

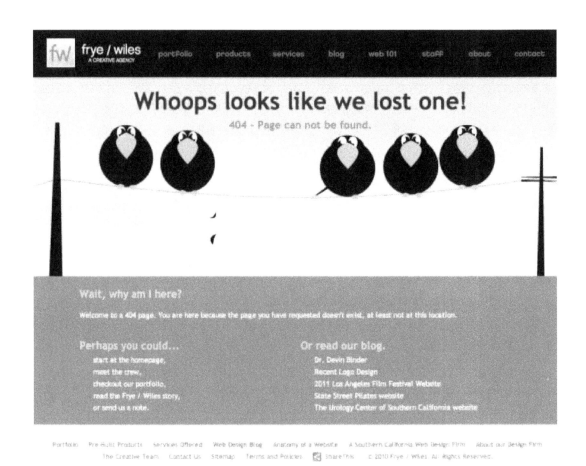

Figure 4.7: Great example of an error-404 page

With or without www

It is important to make sure that your website is accessible with or without www. The problem is that you need to make the webpage called www.yourdomain.com at all times, so if people click http://yourdomain.com they will simply get a 301 redirect which you have installed, so you avoid loosing ranking on the split between the domain with or without www.

It is easy to change the .htaccess file on your server so you avoid that mistake. Simply add the following line in your .htaccess file:

```
RewriteEngine On
RewriteCond %{HTTP_HOST} ^www.YourDomain.com$ [NC]
RewriteRule ^(.*)$ http://YourDomain.com/$1 [R=301,L]
```

That's all you need to do to avoid loosing point with your domain name.

Use Robots.txt to avoid certain content to be public

Use the robots.txt file to control which directories and files on your web server that a search engine would publish for their customers. It in a geeky language means that Robots Exclusion Protocol (REP)-compliant search engine crawler (aka a robot or bot) is permitted to access these files that you didn't exclude. You can also implement a crawl delay to scale back bot crawling activity and establish a pointer to your XML-based Sitemap. Here are examples of coding that you can use for Robots.txt.

Allow indexing of everything
- User-agent: *
- Disallow:

Disallow indexing of everything
- User-agent: *
- Disallow: /

Disallow Googlebot from indexing of a folder, except for allowing the indexing of one file in that folder
- User-agent: Googlebot
- Disallow: /folder1/
- Allow: /folder1/myfile.html

Tip: Go to www.robotstxt.org for more information and examples about Robots

Avoid iframes

iFrames are a big NO-NO for you to use in general on your website, for that simple reasons that you directly have chosen to miss out a great ranking. When you use an iFrame your URL does not allow to change or show and that way the user and the search engine cannot capture the content. The biggest problems with iFrames are that you do not get any incoming links from people endorsing your site, and as you know that is crucial when it comes to rankings so be aware of that!

Avoid Flash

Flash is currently not a W3 standard and elements, such as Header Tags, simply do not exist for the search engines to evaluate what a site is about. For that simple reason they have a tough time evaluating your site and you would often be lead out of the search engines. Currently Google has the most advanced methods of crawling Flash, yet it is still seemingly unable to:

- Read text as symbols (VERY IMPORTANT)
- Follow links (although it can at least find deep links through swfaddress which is located in the flash file if being used)
- Make sense of and determine the weight of specific content (Adobe has not provided any new standard that W3 could accept and has no feature to mimic currently accepted tags that search engines could adopt)

Even though your flash content is optimized would immediately eliminate up to 20% of your potential search audience, so why to include flash when new standards such as JQuery and HTML5 makes your SEO easier?

Make a Sitemap

If you open a Google Webmaster account, the first Google will ask you is a sitemap for your website. A Sitemap makes indexing of your site by the search engines a smother process. In other words, it helps the search engines find all the pages on your site. Some websites only have a few of their pages in the search engines and this can be due to poor linking, lack of a Sitemap or a chunk of other reasons. Safe bet is to create a sitemap that links to all of the major sections of your website. If you have a small website, linking to all the pages is a good idea. Web-crawlers will thank you for making their busy life's easier. It provides PageRank or link popularity to all pages it links to. Remember don't underestimate your own internal links pointing to your own pages. A sitemap can become another source of quality links with descriptive text for your own pages. What you should be aware of when creating a sitemap:

- A Sitemap should not exchange Google's invisible robot's navigation structure, but it should just be to support it.
- Avoid XML sitemaps, many companies have lost important ranks from the use of XML sitemaps.
- Make sure your sitemap uses the proper search keywords in the links.
- Make a nice, need and easy to understand sitemap, your users might need it.

Finally go to www.google.com/webmasters/tools/ and submit your sitemap as well.

Important to use the right ISP (Web Host)

It matters where you host your website and if you pick a provider in Europe when your target market is the US, you will miss out points in your PageRank. The search engines would look at the servers location and estimate since you are located in lets say Germany, it must be were your main business is located, therefore your ranking in the US will suffer. Sometimes people do shared hosting, which is cheap compared to a dedicated server. The problem is if someone on your server since you are sharing same IP address, that do spamming and other activates that Google would Black List, they would actually end up punishing you as well even though you have all the best intentions in the world. So beware were you host location wise and if you share or have a dedicated server!

Did you learn the following?

☐ I know that redirect 301 is important if I do changes

☐ I feel that I Understand all the basic principles of SEO at this point?

☐ I understand that hosting matters

☐ I know what a 404-error page is and why it appears

☐ I know how to avoid Duplicate Content and know it cost PageRank if I forget to do so!

☐ I know that Flash, iFrames etc is a big NO-NO!

Own Notes:

_____

_____

_____

_____

_____

_____

_____

Part

3

Measuring the effects of your

SEO efforts!

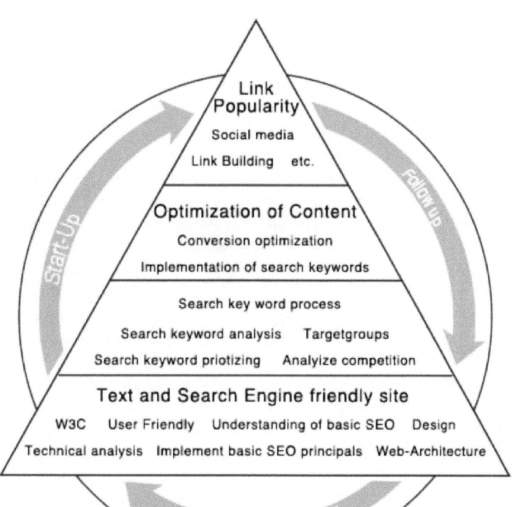

CHAPTER

8

"As any other business process, would you need to follow up on your SEO efforts"

8:// Follow up on your SEO efforts!

Following up on your SEO efforts is important and SEO is an ongoing process that you need to focus on, if you want to be number one. The great thing about following up, you would quickly realize how well your SEO efforts have paid off. Doing a research on your SEO efforts will quickly give you an indication what you need to focus on.

Important measurements for your SEO efforts

There are three overall ways to check your ranking on the search engines and what your SEO efforts have paid:

*	Your current rank in the search engines.
*	Sales/Conversion rates from SEO efforts.
*	Traffic/Visitors gained from SEO efforts.

You can actually measure all three areas online by simple research, Google Analytics and a few other methods to measure the above.

Check your ranking on Search Engines

A simple check on the keywords you have focused on will show you how well you have performed with your SEO efforts. The only problem is this process is long and will take you an awful long time to complete. There do exist a huge quantity of software that either is free or subscription based that you would be able to buy into and it will do the work for you. Use of a Rank checker is a great choice and here are a few examples on the ones that are widely used today:

- **SEOmoz Pro** – a service from www.seomoz.org, which measure all parts of your ranking and SEO efforts (monthly subscription required)
- **Rank Checker** – a free plugin for Firefox internet browser which is free and easy to use go to http://tools.seobook.com/firefox/rank-checker.
- **Rank Tracker** – a simple piece of software that you have to download on www.digital-point.com/rank-tracker/.

Advice: Remember to compare your rank with the most widely used words, that you competitors use to compare with them!

Rank Checker:

Since Rank Checker is free, I know most people would consider the tool for that simple fact, and that it is a great tool as well. It is a plugin for your Firefox Internet Browser so it will run simultaneously when you use the browser and it works for Google, Bing and Yahoo!

It is quite easy to install

1.   Open Firefox and if you don't have a Firefox browser installed you can simply do it by clicking on to www.firefox.com

2.   Click on to http://tools.seobook.com/firefox/rank-checker and click download now

3.   A window will show where you have to press install as illustrated below

4. After installation you need to add the domain and the keywords you wish to use after that simply press start

5. After that you will be able to see the results as illustrated, and if you do not

Google Analytics

Google Analytics is most likely one of the best tools for any person in business that owns a webpage. The insight that you can review and track with Google Analytics is outstanding and truly a tool you need to use if you haven't started yet! Google Analytics gives you the absolute inside about what keywords people have searched on when they arrived to your site, it tells you if people leaves and what pages they often leaves your page from, where they are from and we can go on with the functions. But all these datasets that you will generate from Google Analytics is worth a lot for you if you use it the right way, and yes picking search key words from that data set should be done. To install Google Analytics is fairly easy and you should do the following:

1.   Go to www.google.com/analytics sign in with your Google account or open one.

2.   Sign up for a website fill out the info they ask for as illustrated here

3. Copy paste the code and install it to every page on your website, blog or web presence

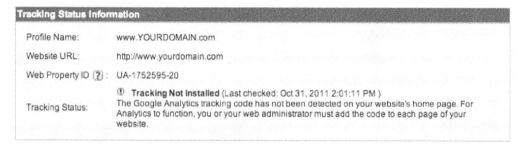

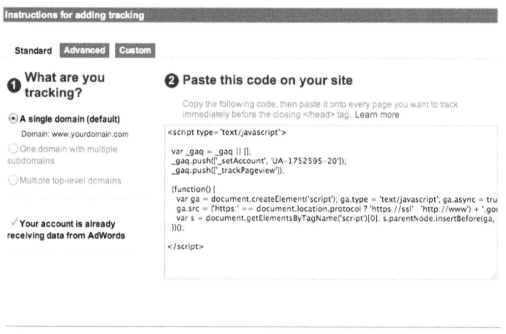

4. That's it and you will be ready to see your results in about 24 hours after installation (and Google updates the data sets for you every 24 hours)

What does Google Analytics offer?

What does Google Analytics offer?

As I mentioned what you can track with Google Analytics is almost endless, and extremely valuable for you. Here is an illustration for the results for a dog kennel in Denmark what we can track immediately (I used the newest version of Google Analytics which is going live now):

Here is an example of number of Visitors, Unique visitors (meaning the actual number of different people), page views, number of pages viewed per visitor and finally the bounce rate which means how many people leave the site right away. Below is an example of the search keywords people used to enter cabaka.com

From this list is the answer obvious, Cabaka is the most widely used key word, while a competitive Kennel, Kennel Nikara actually brings them traffic. If we look at referrals, which is the sites linking to you and are the extremely important part of link building would the data look like the following on the next page:

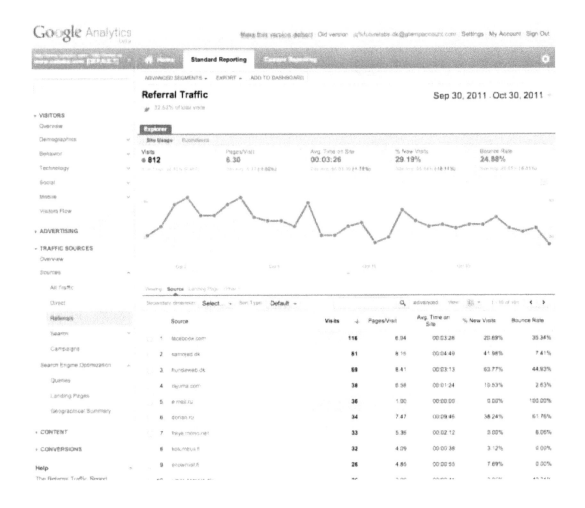

With data like these, is it obvious that you quickly are able to track who is generating traffic for you, which is obvious that it means $$$ and ranking as well. These are just some of the core functions and most basics ones that you should know. If you log on to www.growwinners.com would you be able to see and buy seminars that show you all Google Analytics can do by video, and I highly recommend you to do so!

(Hint turn to the next page)

Did you learn the following?

☐ Do you have an understanding of why you need to use Google Analytics?

☐ You know how to find out your search engine ranking? (hint: Page Rank)

☐ You know how to focus your SEO efforts to a further extend?

Own Notes:

_____

_____

_____

_____

_____

_____

_____

_____

CHAPTER

9

"Why Social media is a part of your new universe!"

9:// Social media is changing the marketplace

Let's look at the real world when it comes to Social Media, there are basically two camps. There are the ones that claim "I don't have time for Social Networking". I also hear "Facebook is for kids". Well that statement is clearly wrong, and if you look at huge founders like Richard Branson (Virgin) and Mark Benioff (Salesforce.com) are among a few names that actively utilize the unique position of communicating with their peers, crowd and customers. On the other hand is there a camp that are completely for Social Media and they tend to believe that it is the answer to any company's prayer. Well that is not entirely true either you do not offer the right products which will cause that you never sell anything. So that leads us all to an easy question why should I invest in social media and what exactly would it do for me?

First of all the point that most business owners fail to see is that Social Media and Social Networking sites have a great impact on their search results. Both Google and Bing have publicly admitted that shares on Facebook and Twitter (and now Google+) have a direct impact on ranking results, so when we want to increase your search results. Both Google and Bing have publicly admitted that shares on Facebook and Twitter (and now Google+) have a direct impact on ranking results, so when we want to increase your search engine optimization would social media be the place to opt-out? (HINT: NO!)

Secondly it is a great channel to interact with customers, and they feel the company is closer to them and listens, which brings the loyalty up to date. When you engage with your customers you would if you do it right, be able to Crowdsource with them and actually speed up your internal Innovation process.

Social media and SEO

Example: You share something relevant to your business on your Facebook Page and Twitter profile.

*   User 1 comes along and "likes" your post
*   User 2 comes along and shares your post (reposts it on their wall and/or re-tweets it on the Twitter profile)
*   User 3 re-tweets user 2's post
*   Users 4 – 20 see the Facebook post that user 2 shared and visits, likes and reads your Facebook Page.
*   Users 13 – 19 share that same post on their Facebook page

I believe you get the idea. By sharing in the social hemisphere, you generated a bunch of inbound links and introduced your business to a number of potential buyers who had no prior knowledge of you. (Though the incoming links do not count much in SEO terms, would the visit from a customer on the other hand matter!) Participation in social networking does increase your odds of being consistently found at the top of the search engines. Think about it Google do emphasize on Google+ and the more people who clicks Plus (Like in Facebook terms the more authority you would gain on Google and that equals ranking credits.

One rule of thumb like you do in any other channel of you business, in social media realm, you have to practice reciprocity. In other words, don't be there to just post about your self. Make sure you share relevant content from other people in your networks, to gain trust, award people for sharing your work, make it viral etc. Con sider the difference between a link farm (low quality, Don't go there) to a web site and a content rich, authoritative (high quality) site. If you do share quality from your users, they would share your or in other words if you provide them with information they like, they will spread your brand name like a firestorm.

Social Marketing is something every business owner needs to make time for and work. The bottom line is, your SEO plan is incomplete without including a Social Element.

The Social Media World

Facebook:
In less than seven years, Facebook has managed to gain more than 750 million users, which makes them the biggest social media network on the planet. Facebook has more members than the United States or the European Union have residents (Facebook.com, 2011). Facebook has a large advantage from its strong user base and the amount of time users are spending on their platform—which has made it the online platform people spend the most time using on average (Comcast, 2011). The unique thing about Facebook is that companies can access users easily through a social acquisition, and when people spread something by word-to-mouth it is strongly effective on the platform.

Twitter:
Twitter, in its recent years, has become extremely popular—especially in the U.S.—and has become the network for breaking news, such as when the revolution in

Egypt happened recently a lot of people about it through Twitter. In March 2011, Twitter reached its milestone of 200 million users (Twitter, 2011). Twitter is a different social network than others since everything is limited to 140 characters or fewer. Twitter is another tool that can utilize and/or conduct information from users to engage in crowdsourcing.

Google+:

Google+ is the newest platform in the social media scene, and is maybe one of the most ambitious launches from Google in their history. A famous Silicon Valley venture capitalist, Bill Gross, announced on his Twitter stream that he believes that Google+ would be the fastest growing network to reach 100 million users. Google+ is relatively new since it is not open for the public yet, since it is operating by invitation only at this stage. Google+ could become very important for companies in the future, since the platform is also depending on people's search habits, and is recommending in search results what your network likes, which would potentially influence data collecting from different groups of the future.

Vkontakte (Russia)

Vkontakte is Russia's biggest social media network, with a user base of 135 million as of February 2011. Vkontakte is a very powerful tool to collect information from the old USSR countries, and since Russia is a part of the "BRIC" countries, the net work's growth is expected to continue to increase over time. Reaching the Russian population when addressing their demographic and their culture is important, but like any other network, Vkontakte losing users to Facebook.

Orkut (South American, part of Google)

Orkut is the biggest social media network of Latin America, but like Vkontakte they are losing members to Facebook. Orkut has around 100 Million active members and Google owns them, so it would be no big surprise if Orkut is later integrated into Google+, and that might be a strong reason for them to stay in business against Facebook.

Tencent (China)

Tencent is the second-biggest social media network in the world, after Facebook, and most people in the western countries might never have heard about the site. Tencent, as December 2010, had more than 640 million members, making it at one point bigger than Facebook. Tencent is the biggest social network in Asia and the best connection to the crowd in that part of the world. It is a publicly traded company, and it really focuses on being the number one social network in Mainland China. Facebook is rumored to make a partnership with Baidu, the Chinese version of Google, to enter the market and compete against Tencent.

When engaging in social media, it is important to target the right network and the ones that are suitable for your business. Are you in music? Then Myspace is still one of the networks you would wish to use. If you were targeting China, you might want to consider Tencent, and for Russia Vkontakte. But picking the right network and figuring out a winning strategy is essential. A great example of one company that did well with social media is Virgin America: the company become notorious for its engagement with their customers through social media, and is one of the most responsive to customer's requests or complaints through Twitter and Facebook at this point.

(Hint turn to the next page)

Did you learn the following?

☐ The social media matters
☐ That there are other channels, besides Facebook
☐ Russia and China have to major networks

Own Notes:

_____

_____

_____

_____

_____

_____

_____

_____

_____

SEO

DEFINITIONS

"If something didn't make sense, or you just feel like learning new technical terms"

10:// SEO Definitions

301 redirect - URL redirection or domain forwarding

algorithm - the mathematical formula in a search engine used to rank sites

anchor text - the text that is clickable. Also known as hyperlink

backlinks - a word for incoming links to a website

black hat SEO - unethical high-risk techniques used to gain good rank that do not follow search engine guidelines. Some examples are hiding written text (black letters on black background), link farming and cloaking

blogroll - a list of links, usually placed in the sidebar of a blog, that reads as a list of recommendations by the host of the blog

dofollow - a term for standard incoming links that do not have the nofollow attribute

Firefox - a web browser developed by Mozilla that is free to download and provides an alternative to Microsoft's Windows Internet Explorer

frames - website design using multiple, independent sections to create a single webpage. Each frame is built as a separate HTML file, but with one "master" file to identify each selection. [unfriendly to engine crawlers]

Google Analytics - a free service offered by Google that generates detailed stats about website visitors.

A benefit of using Google Analytics is to check the Page Views your site gets, to determine pay-per-click and other paid ads quality. Other benefits include tracking: Keyword popularity specific to a search engine, all other referring websites and visitors' physical location

googlebot - Google software that collects documents from the web to build a searchable index for their search engine

HTML - HyperText Markup Language. Designed for the creation of webpages with clickable text and other information to be displayed in a web browser

HTML validator - a tool used to check an HTML document for various write-up problems.

http - hypertext transfer protocol: Transfers information between servers and browsers

https - Hypertext Transfer Protocol Secure: Transfers encrypted info

image alt tag - the alternative text that the browser displays when the website visitor does not want to or cannot see an image on a website. Placed in the image tag like this: <img src="seo.gif" alt="SEO">

inlink - another word for backlink

internal pages - inside pages

IP address - Internet Protocol address. A unique identifier that has four numbers separated by dots, like this: 57.247.271.73. All computers across the internet are assigned one. They are used like street addresses.

keyword - a significant word in a web page's content, url address or backlink titles that indicates its subject

link farm - a group of links on a variety of pages solely for the purpose of increasing link popularity for search engines. Link farms are normally created by programs, rather than by human beings. [an engine penalty]

link popularity - the number and quality of inbound links pointing to a given web page

META tags - write-up placed within the HTML <head> </head> tags of a webpage, providing informationthat is not visible to browsers

nofollow - an HTML attribute used to instruct search engines that a hyperlink should not influence the link target's engine ranking. Used to cut down on irrelevant content to improve the quality of search engine results.

The nofollow tag looks like:
1) <head> <meta name="robots" content="noindex, nofollow"> </head> and
2) <a href="http://___/" rel="nofollow"></a>.

To Check for Nofollow Tag: At web page, View > Source, click Edit, Find, then type nofollow. When there are no nofollows on the page, that's all that needs to be done. When finding a nofollow:
1) Were the head tags already searched?
2) Finding your url will show if it has the tag.

organic SEO - techniques used for unpaid high ranking results on search engines

SE - search engine

SEM - search engine marketing

SEO - search engine optimization

social network - a website designed to create online communities focused around common interests or a way for people to communicate

unethical SEO - using search optimization techniques that do not fall within all engine's guidelines

URL - Uniform Resource Locator. A world wide web address

web hosting service - a company that provides web server space to individuals and organizations, used to store all of a website's files. That server hosts the web site.

white hat SEO - techniques for high rank that follow search engine guidelines

XML - Extensible Markup Language

About the Author

Jesper is Author of a Winners DNA and he is a highly educated winner with an MBA in Management from Nova Southeastern University and a Master of Science in Management of Innovation and Business Development from Copenhagen Business School.

Jesper Qvist is an accomplished entrepreneur with a huge knowledge base about entrepreneurship and strategy, which he is sharing in his first book, A Winners DNA. Jesper is originally from Denmark but lives in Miami Beach, Florida.

Twitter: @Jqvist
Facebook: www.facebook.com/JesperQvistAuthor
Web: www.AWinnersDNA.com
              www.JesperQvist.com
              www.growwinners.com

www.ingramcontent.com/pod-product-compliance
Lightning Source LLC
Chambersburg PA
CBHW060134060326
40690CB00018B/3870